ADVANCED PRAISE FOR *TIME IS TIGHT*

Time is Tight is an amazingly challenging book. Its most refreshing aspect is the reversing educational approach which brings forward educational strategies from "developing" countries which might have some bearing on problems and issues rampant in the rich and overpowering "developed" societies. The differential aspect is the more human and holistic conception which liberation struggles facilitated in countries recently breaking the yoke of colonialism. Contrary to the mercantilistic western societies, an appreciation and respect for the person as a unique cultural human being still remains a plausible option in the African societies mirrored in the book. Additionally, Meyer makes a further contribution by debunking the prevailing unidirectional flow of information from the haves to the have-nots and, also, by helping to shatter the myth of the replicability of the western educational schemes in the Third World. The covert ideological basis behind those efforts is but to assure the further continuation of oppression and the new faces of colonialism. I strongly recommend this book.

-Luis Nieves Falcon, Professor Emeritus, University of Puerto Rico

In *Time is Tight*, Matt Meyer gives a new dimension to multicultural education, as well as, body and specificity to the disembodied, often vague concept of transformation. Unlike other critics, Meyer upholds an assertion that significant change in American education is not only very much needed but possible by pointing to sources of inspiration and example. In acknowledging flaws in the educational renewals in Eritrea and South Africa, he renders these cases practical and real sources of useful examples rather than impractical, ideal models. The cases are heartening: evidence that the United States has something to learn from other countries, most significantly and–perhaps surprising to the culturally myopic–from Africa. The book is a constructive contribution toward overcoming that myopia in educational practice, and, we might hope, toward the politics of transformation to a more just world.

-Betty A. Reardon, Founding Director, Teachers College Peace Education Center, Columbia University

Americans expect to view the world as exotic at best, with vast expanses of backwardness and blank emptiness in every corner. Matt Meyer, an American scholar and student of Africa, performs a neat reversal here: he takes us to Africa in order to look back with a renewed sense of purpose and a more clearly articulated strategy. The lessons are vast and deep. Meyer shows us what education has meant–and might yet mean–in humanity's ongoing quest for social justice. In *Time is Tight* the two great lamps that light the path of humanistic education–enlightenment and liberation–are seen anew, and amped up for the struggle to come.

-Bill Ayers, Distinguished Professor of Education, University of Illinois at Chicago

Matt Meyer has presented us with a comparative, thoroughly researched study of the Education for Liberation struggle from Eritrea, South Africa, and the United States. The book also explores the alternative cultural and national philosophies underpinning these struggles of Africans or people of African origin confronting the historical white or colonial hegemonies of the educational practice in these countries. His account of the significant influences on the ongoing transformation of education in South Africa that has accompanied to date its political process towards a nonracial democracy is detailed and well documented.

-Neil McGurk, Director, Sacred Heart College Research and Development Unit, South Africa

Through education and interaction with students and youth, fresh minds and future leaders, one can have major influence in liberating the mind and bringing change in society if done properly and responsibly. The Eritrean struggle for independence was carried out by students and the youth with the support of the entire population. Matt Meyer's *Time is Tight* captures the Eritrean spirit during our struggle. Meyer brings to light what transpired in the middle of harsh reality–war and constant bombings, displacement, flight and constant movement, and shortage of practically everything that would normally make education possible. Meyer also shows the human spirit, determination and dedication for change and progress through education that was a bright spot in the Eritrean struggle for self-determination. Education was indeed a very important liberating process during the years of armed struggle, a hope abandoned by the current government. In *Time is Tight*, Meyer compares educational policies during the struggle for liberation in South Africa and Eritrea, relating these experiences to that of the U.S. through stories about his own connection to and experience with U.S. educational policy and practice. It is remarkable how Meyer relates his own life experiences, and the lessons he's learned, to the ongoing struggles for social justice, liberation, and solidarity. I admire Meyer's profound understanding of education and its transformative power in the lives of individuals and societies. A copy of *Time is Tight* is displayed prominently amongst my books.

-Paulos Tesfagiorgis, leading member of the Constitutional Convention of Eritrea; Director of Justice Africa; recipient of the 2003 Rafto Prize for Human Rights

Time Is Tight

TIME IS TIGHT

Urgent Tasks for Educational Transformation
Eritrea, South Africa, and the U.S

Matt Meyer

Africa World Press, Inc.

P.O. Box 1892　　　　P.O. Box 48
Trenton, NJ 08607　　　　　　Asmara, ERITREA

Africa World Press, Inc.

P.O. Box 1892 P.O. Box 48
Trenton, NJ 08607 Asmara, ERITREA

Copyright © 2007 Matt Meyer
First Printing 2007

All rights reserved. No part of this publication may be reproduced, stored in a retrieval system or transmitted in any form or by any means electronic, mechanical, photocopying, recording or otherwise without the prior written permission of the publisher.

Book design: Saverance Publishing Services (SPS)
Cover design: Ashraful Haque and SPS

Library of Congress Cataloging-in-Publication Data

Meyer, Matt.
  Time is tight : urgent tasks for educational transformation : Eritrea, South Africa, and the U.S. / Matt Meyer.
    p. cm.
  ISBN 1-59221-478-9 (hard back) -- ISBN 1-59221-479-7 (pbk.)
  1. Education--Eritrea. 2. Educational change--Eritrea. 3. Education--South Africa. 4. Educational change--South Africa. 5. Education--United States. 6. Educational change--United States. I. Title. II. Title: Urgent tasks for educational transformation.

LA1521.M49 2006
370.9635--dc22
                           2006009701

Children of the Soil,
pull up your socks
for the time is tight.

They are not yet aware
siyaya ... siyaya ...

Siyaya, siyaya,
Where we know ...

Fulfilling the once assigned mission,
Baba, forward we are going,
Never shall we retreat
For the drumbeat of Africa has beaten.

> — excerpt from the 1982 poem "Time Is Tight" by Mojaki Thulo, student of the African National Congress Solomon Mahlango Freedom College ("Siyaya" roughly translates from the Xhosa as "we go forward.")

This book is humbly dedicated to the following unrecognized teachers of the world:

- the youth of independent Africa — especially Eritrea and South Africa — who struggle now for freedom from want;

- the youth of not-yet-independent Puerto Rico — and all of the nations currently enslaved by the modern drive to maintain empires and imperialism;

- the over one hundred U.S. political prisoners/POWs and prisoners of conscience, who fight, despite continued incarceration, for basic recognition, survival, and amnesty and for the human rights of all people.

TABLE OF CONTENTS

Acknowledgements	xv
Foreward	xix
Introduction: Education for Liberation	1

Section I: Educational Apartheid: Education under Fire

Chapter 1: "Outsiders" — Contemporary Education in the U.S.	13
Chapter 2: We Have Our Voices: Eritrea in the Pre-independence Era	23
Chapter 3: Time Is Tight: Education in South Africa under Apartheid	31
Chapter 4: Positive and Negative Globalisms	39

Section II: Educational Alternatives

Chapter 5: Pan-Africanism and Africanist Philosophies of Education	49
Chapter 6: An Additional "R": Reconciliation— Education, and Empowerment in Postapartheid South Africa	59
Chapter 7: Eritrea at Ten: Victories and Realities	93
Chapter 8: Working within the U.S. Pressure Cooker	119
Conclusion: Learning from Africa: Teaching about Human Rights in the U.S.	157
Appendix: Whose Standards? An African Test	167
Endnotes	171
Index	195

ACKNOWLEDGEMENTS

To be a successful teacher, one must, as has been noted, first and foremost be a student. I am privileged to have had three outstanding teacher-mentors, who deserve more thanks then I can ever say. Dr. Luis Nieves Falcon and Bill Sutherland have opened up whole worlds to me, as well as welcoming me into their personal lives. Mawina Sowa Kouyate took the time and effort, when I was beginning my political and professional journeys as a very young adult, to help hone my analysis and build a strategic element to the actions I took.

My international travels and studies have always been made richer by the wealth of people who have taken time out of their own busy schedules to host, meet with, and generally take care of me. Many of those interviewed for this work have been cited in the text, so I will not repeat their names here: but I am grateful to them all. Others deserving of mention are, in Eritrea, Abrehet Goytom, Arefaine Tewolde, and Jeffrey Shannon. In South Africa, special thanks to Nozizwe Madlala Routledge, MP; Neil Mitchell; and Dr. Ivan Toms.

In the U.S., I have, for well over a decade, enjoyed the support of Sherry Zekowski, a local instructional superintendent with the New York City Department of Education's Region Eight. She has provided a special style of leadership — truly encouraging the best in those around her. Evelyn Kalibala of the Office of Multicultural Education has been both a friend as well as an inspiration. The original impetus of this book took place during a yearlong sabbatical: a professional practice that serves to refresh and deepen the knowledge base of long-term teachers, one now in danger of being eliminated in contract negotiations. Superintendents Stephen Phillips and Richard Organisciak and Deputy Superintendent Margaret Bing-Wade helped nurture my career up till the point of sabbatical; Deputy Superintendents Alan Warner and Elayna Konstan and teacher Molly N'Tulli reviewed early outlines of a sabbatical project that helped inspire this work.

Many colleagues have challenged me and made my life easier by their own good work; I will name but a few who are not already mentioned in the text: Linda Allocca, Leon Arredondo, UFT vice president Frank Carucci, Husana Diabi, Rosalind Francis, Jerry Long, Judith Hemans, principal Joan Indart, Stephanie Francis, Arlene Hinds, Henry Lyons, Veronica Romero, Aarti Sawhney, and Paul Surovell. Educators for Social Responsibility staff member and longtime War Resisters League comrade Sam Diener allowed me to share some ideas about *Time Is Tight;* Peace and Justice Studies Association executive director Simona Sharoni helped provide a forum for the research contained herein. At the final stages of this book's production, three longtime colleagues—Dr. Brenda Greene, John Judge and Paul Magno—lent their special assistance and support.

I am indebted to two early readers of the manuscript: Bill Ayers, director of the Center for Youth and Society at the University of Illinois at Chicago, and Leslie Agard-Jones, dean of the College of Education at William Peterson University, New Jersey. The members of my local collective, Resistance in Brooklyn, also played a major role: in addition to the RnB teachers interviewed in the text, I must thank Betsy Mickel and Bob Lederer for their assistance with typing, copy-editing, and general commentary. Liz Roberts and Colin Starger continue to help me make sense of this crazy moment in time. Elspeth Meyer, an early childhood educator, has been a lifelong role model in many areas. My lifelong friend and comrade Jonathan Cohen, who helped encourage this book but passed away while it was still in progress, continues to provide guidance; his indomitable spirit is a sustaining one. Betsy deserves a second shout-out; her final careful eye set this manuscript on a steady course to completion. Proofreader/Educators Aarti Sawhney and Jenny Radke gave it a final review.

As mentioned previously, my own path toward teaching as a profession was undoubtedly paved by my father, Simon Meyer, and family members Marilyn Meyer, Sylvia Meyer, and

Mollie Lehrenbaum. They have more than earned my profound gratitude and love.

Time Is Tight would not have been possible without the consistent support, reflections, and friendship of Africa World Press's Kassahun Checole. His contributions are many — to my own education and to the many fields and disciplines he works in.

Finally, my life partner, teacher-extraordinaire and author Meg Starr, continues to provide a practical, political, and personal base for my life's works. I can think of no person more responsible for constantly challenging me to look deeper at the complexities of any given situation; her subsequent support fills me with energy and hope. Our son, Michael Del, reminds me on a daily basis that our work, by definition, can never be fully complete. His joy, curiosity, and passion teach me, once again, that the world can indeed have a bright future.

FOREWORD
by Ela Gandhi, Member of Parliament (ANC), South Africa; granddaughter of Mohandas K. Gandhi

Reading through this manuscript brought back memories of the '70s and '80s when we grappled with the issues of apartheid education in South Africa. It was a period when Education Crisis Committees were being set up all over the country to protect our children, who were being harassed by the police and the authorities, and to look at alternate education from the apartheid education that was being forced upon our children.

Many of the debates recorded in this book were debates that we grappled with in the National Education Crisis Committee, when we set out to develop an Education Charter. Those were repressive times, and education was used to suppress the oppressed people of South Africa. The distorted interpretations of our history, of economics, of sociology and health, revealed how education in the hands of a corrupt government can destroy a whole generation.

We began to appreciate the value of real education, of truth, of access, and of methodology. People could be easily enslaved by a dictatorial methodology that takes away the power from the people, that leaves a feeling of inadequacy in some and a false sense of superiority in others. The psychology of the oppressed was fast taking root in our society, and we had to eliminate it before it destroyed us.

Time Is Tight is an important piece of literature for educators all over the world. It illustrates some of the basic and fundamental points of departure in a new system of education, away from the past dominant culture syndrome to a forward-looking, holistic approach geared toward the development of society, of community, of values, and of a new culture.

We need literature from Africa and about Africa to inform our work, not simply because we want an Afrocentric system, nor because we reject everything that comes from the West, but because a great deal that has happened in South Africa and Africa has been trashed, forgotten, and not given the prominence that it deserves. We need to relocate all the best models and practices of our forefathers.

If education is to produce a new generation of empowered people, then we need to support literature such as presented in this inspiring book.

INTRODUCTION: EDUCATION FOR LIBERATION

After an hour or two, but long before we've allowed the group to "gel" — to truly come together and feel comfortable with one another — we tell the teachers to take out a piece of paper for a little quiz. Nothing — not the self-effacing nature of the phrase "little quiz," not my own brand of New York sarcasm evident to most participants during the first moments of our meeting hours earlier, not the fact that these trained test-givers and curriculum designers must understand on some level that a quiz given in the first section of a graduate course would likely "count" for little of their final grade — nothing diminishes people's nervous, giggly reaction. We tell them to number the pages one through ten and await further instructions. The routineness of the task only seems to intensify the nervousness.

The Multicultural Lists Activity,[1] designed by a colleague and me in the early 1990s to serve as part of the New York City Board of Education in-service teacher-training course, "An Introduction to Education That Is Multicultural," was developed primarily to demonstrate to graduate- and postgraduate-level professionals that there is much we don't know, much we still have to learn from one another and from our students and the communities around us. This teacher-as-learner concept, so fundamental to the philosophy of education for liberation, often seems the hardest to confront people with in practical ways. Even in a city as diverse as New York, with experienced and tenured teachers numbering in the tens of thousands, there are still vast amounts of information that even the most politically progressive or multiculturally minded must seek out, search for, and continue to absorb. So we give them a quiz: ruffle some feathers, release the tension with some humor, make a point or two.

"After the numbers one and two," I intone — in my deepest, most male and mock-serious voice — "simply write the names of any two famous, contemporary African Americans, living or dead." This is easy, teachers are writing, I'm circling the room, "very good," "oh, interesting," chiding people not to copy from one another, answering a few over-intellectualized questions about the true definition of "famous" for those wondering what the catch will be. "Under the numbers three and four," I continue, "two famous, contemporary Latino Americans." Slight hesitations; now some are asking how broad the definition of "contemporary" can be — but most are writing, self-satisfied, playing the game. We haven't even gone through the complete "What's in a Name?" exercise,[2] discussing the debates between the terms "Latino" and "Hispanic"; that comes later. For now, I begin to hurry along. "After numbers five and six, write the names of two famous, contemporary Asian Americans." Always some pauses here. I wait. "For seven and eight, two famous contemporary Native Americans." Pens drop. Enlightened educators, who know that they already know all they had to know about multiculturalism, begin to look a bit unhappy — they've figured out the catch. "Finally, for nine and ten, give me two famous, contemporary European Americans." Some are writing, but most are now ready to process — with incomplete lists two-thirds filled out. Multicultural lists is my game — so I get to make the rules. With strict, though caricatured, adherence to a "don't look at your neighbor's paper" policy, I rattle off some last-minute rule changes. If, under numbers one and two, people have written any of the following names, I instruct the class that they must discard them as "too obvious" and replace them with others. Too quickly, I read off "Reverend Martin Luther King, Malcolm X, Colin Powell, Jesse Jackson, Al Sharpton, Michael Jackson," and a few others who may be particularly typical at the moment. Latino athletes are to be removed, as are Asians in the entertainment industry. Since very few people have written anything in the Native American category, I simply emphasize the need for twentieth-century figures. ("They haven't *all* been killed off, you know!") So Pocahontas, usually the number one vote-getter, has to go, as does Geronimo. I leave the ones who have struggled to figure out the names of naturalized U.S. citizens who were born in Europe (Henry Kissinger and Zbigniew Brzezinski are always high on the list) alone with their struggles.

The game ends noisily, as we all process who's left on the lists. People are anxious to share their names and the mini-biographies of the interesting people they've come up with. Only a couple of staff people in an average class of twenty participants will have all ten names. We learn from each other about those categories in which we are weakest. Since our "average" group in New York City is already somewhat ethnically diverse, the point is clear that we each do still have things to learn — and the class proceeds from there. That the exercise deals only with race and ethnicity, that it only focuses on heroes and the famous, is of little concern at this starting point. Some defenses have been slightly diffused, some information exchanged. For our under-represented indigenous peoples category, I try to elicit the name of the jailed American Indian Movement leader for whom over thirty members of Congress, half a dozen Nobel Peace Prize laureates, and over five million petitioners have called for amnesty. Still, few have heard of U.S. political prisoner Leonard Peltier.[3] Some now know the name of Native American environmentalist Winona LaDuke, who ran in 2000 as the vice presidential candidate on the Green Party ticket. If I'm in an ambitious mood, and we haven't run out of time, I push the conversation a little further and ask about the gender balance of the "final ten" on people's lists. Sexual orientation is rarely raised. But teachers have begun to think and to talk to one another about their thinking process.

* * *

Perhaps the most disturbing — and revealing — aspect of the multicultural lists exercise, as I reflect on ten years of conducting it for in-service and graduate courses, is the confused and confusing way in which educators understand (or misunderstand) the concepts "African" and "European." Believing that teachers are, in general, reflective of the educated population at large, I am struck but not surprised at the invisible nature of the ethnicities of white folk. Because of centuries of white supremacy, our European heritage has become — more often than not — redundant. So whites are never "European Americans," but simply "Americans."

This, of course, does not mean that — in a callous attempt to pretend that a level playing field exists and that whites must join the multicultural festival as "equal" participants — there is denial of the heritage of people of European descent. Celebrating Greek or Italian or East European Jewish ethnicities is important and does have a role to play in understanding diversity; there is simply a qualitative and quantitative difference in social power dynamics between people in the U.S. considered white and those considered nonwhite. In this post-civil rights era, the difference between celebrating and claiming one's heritage and understanding one's privileges is, however, all too significant but uncommonly part of collective consciousness. The subtleties between the two are evident, and comedian George Carlin zeroes in on those subtleties in a "short take" of his *Napalm and Silly Putty:* "I don't understand this notion of ethnic pride," he writes, with his typical sarcasm and harshness. "'Proud to be Irish,' 'Puerto Rican pride,' 'Black pride.' It seems to me that pride should be reserved for accomplishments; things you attain or achieve, not things that happen to you by chance. Being Irish isn't a skill; it's genetic. You wouldn't say, 'I'm proud to have brown hair,' or 'I'm proud to be short and stocky.' So why the fuck should you say you're proud to be Irish? I'm Irish, but I'm not particularly proud of it. Just glad! Goddamn glad to be Irish!" [4]

Noel Ignatiev, in his groundbreaking *How the Irish Became White*,[5] details one European American ethnic group's history in accepting the privileges of whiteness — not simply a "given" for a group considered underclass in Europe and upon first arrival in the U.S. Since Ignatiev's publication, critical white studies and critical race studies have become a growing part of academic investigation, as the social construct that is race undergoes a much-needed deconstruction. The conclusions of this work, for Ignatiev and others, however, have led to a sometimes disturbing tendency toward what I would term a wishful-thinking approach.

Calling on so-called whites to become "race traitors," the idea is that — through a belief in the abolition of whiteness and the deconstruction of race — equality and justice can be achieved. Belief alone, unfortunately — even combined with sound academic research — will not shift the paradigms of power. Nor will sensitivity trainings or courses in multiculturalism. Actions, as many of our grandmothers reminded us, speak louder than words, and for many in the New York City school system, the actions of the Oceanhill-Brownsville experiment and subsequent teachers strike over thirty years ago still affect perceptions today. Arguably constituting one of the most divisive and decisive moments in U.S. Black-Jewish relations, these events cemented in many ways the fact of European Jewish, post-World War II "whiteness" within U.S. society.[6] That it happened within the teaching profession puts all the more responsibility on us to be clear today about issues of race and power. For a generation of whites in the school system, in search of progressive alternatives but aware of themselves only as Americans, the question looms large of how to take appropriate antiracist action.

* * *

No one makes the "Brzezinski-Kissinger mistake" with regard to the term African American. Not once has a staff member tried to think of an African-born, naturalized U.S. citizen under that category — though more than a few Caribbean teachers of African descent have wondered about their "qualifications." Does "African American" apply only to those descendants of the northern transatlantic slave trade? These "New Africans," as some have termed the group, certainly share cultures and a history as distinct from contemporaries born in Africa as from others in the diaspora.[7] I have tried, as a teacher-trainer, to focus not on the political correctness of any one term or another, but rather on the need for educators to be sensitive to all of the many terms, labels, organizations, and self-definitions that exist in today's complicated and multifaceted world. Ultimately, though, my thoughts turn back, as a historian and social studies teacher, to the "motherland" of world history — to that most misunderstood Africa.

High school students, in their drive to pass Regents exams, tend to know the basics between countries, cities, and continents. It's the colleagues that really get to me. They describe their plans to travel to Paris and Rome and Africa! Family members confound me as they innocently ask about the weather "down there," forgetting that any place three and one-half times the size of the continental U.S. has no one temperature, no single language or sole political or economic entity. An African educator colleague recently told me of a conversation with the Tanzanian ambassador to the United Nations. "People are always talking about impoverished Africa, Africa at war," noted the ambassador, "when this applies only to fifteen or so countries on the continent. Yet there are over fifty countries that make up Africa, most of them thriving and doing fine!"

A sharper understanding of African social and educational dynamics will not automatically bring forth answers to the burning questions of U.S. race relations or U.S. educational reforms. Nonetheless, when a growing number of U.S. reformers are calling for a greater number of seemingly radical educational transformations, I believe it is necessary to explore the nature of school systems where such changes have at least been attempted. No comparative study can be framed around exact and easily replicable models. One must begin from the point of view of similarities, and the most obvious factors when looking at New York's secondary schools are their diversity, their shortages, and, in the case of the alternative schools and programs, their attempt at community-based, teacher- and student-centered reforms. Another factor to consider, aside from the vastness and sheer logistical intensity of New York City's high schools, is the related systemic stress and duress faced by many within the educational community. This stress is manifest in the consistent presence of violent behavior, constant poverty, class divides, and interethnic conflicts. As we consider these factors, two African nations emerge from which to draw comparison and analysis.[8]

South Africa, a nation rich in mineral and human resources but with extensive poverty as well, has attempted widespread educational reforms since the end of apartheid rule in 1994. Eritrea, the African nation most recently to win full independence in 1993, has had a reputation for its commitment to educational innovations for all. Both countries have had to deal with ethnic strife and issues relating to a multilingual population; both have faced extensive violence. Class and population divisions were fundamental to their colonial and neocolonial legacies. More than any of this, however, South Africans and Eritreans have — in relatively the same period of time, though with significantly different approaches and hurdles — attempted to set forth an education for the liberation of their people. They have done this with official governmental and administrative initiatives, with grassroots and locally based projects, and with mixed successes and setbacks. When we review issues such as literacy studies, use of multiple perspectives, increased access, student- and community-based practices, attentive assessment techniques, and antibias curriculum, we can see that these countries provide relevant case studies for our own past decade of educational change. This work is, first and foremost, an attempt, through a review of South African and Eritrean social and educational transformations, to elicit any meaningful lessons for our current U.S. educational situation — any clues or cures we could learn from the African experience.

* * *

To be sure, my approaches toward educational reform, and the very definitions of education itself, owe much not only to African educational philosophy, but to Latin America as well. Specifically, the work of Brazilian educator Paulo Freire, author of the monumental work *Pedagogy of the Oppressed*,[9] frames many of my own assumptions. Ina Shor, who along with Caroline Pari edited a recent volume on "critical teaching across differences,"[10] has elicited key quotations from Freire, most notably: "Education Is Politics."

In *A Pedagogy for Liberation*, Freire notes that each teacher has to ask, "What kind of politics am I doing in the classroom? That is, in favor of whom am I being a teacher? By asking in favor of whom am I educating, the teacher must also ask against whom am I educating."[11] Disputing that notion that we are somehow politically "neutral," or that teachers must be apolitical to be effective, Freire correctly assesses this impossibility. We may be nonpartisan, and must be open-minded, but our schools are political places and our classrooms are as well. Even a one-on-one interaction between administration and teacher or teacher and student or student and student must be analyzed in the political context within which it occurs.

Another Latin American source of inspiration, and one worthy of reflection upon reviewing the materials presented, is the example of informal popular education that has taken place in Puerto Rico over the past ten years. Campaigns of the most basic nature — going door-to-door, church-to-church, community center-to-community center — have brought about a shift in that island's political orientation. It is useful to note that populist education, even of an informal or overtly political nature, can have truly transformative results.

William Ayers, professor of education and senior university scholar at the University of Illinois at Chicago, and Therese Quinn, in their introduction to the Teachers College Press "Teaching for Social Justice" Series, note that teaching for social justice "might be thought of as a kind of popular education — of, by, and for the people — something that lies at the heart of education in a democracy, education toward a more vital, more muscular democratic society. It can propel us toward action," they add, "away from complacency, reminding us of the powerful commitment, persistence, bravery, and triumphs of our justice-seeking forebears — women and men who sought to build a world that worked for us all."[12] South Africa's anti-apartheid movement, the Eritrean independence movement, the work of Paulo Freire, and the Puerto Rican efforts at decolonization have all been characterized by both detractors and adherents as revolutionary movements. On close inspection, one can understand that each of these movements is fundamentally about a justice-seeking democracy — a radical democracy, perhaps — that guarantees freedom not simply for the majority but minorities, outcasts, and for "the enemy" as well. There are no better challenges to our own U.S.-based educational experiments in democracy than to carefully observe and become students of these global exchanges.

* * *

"Basic education is a human right," stated United Nations Ambassador Per Norstrom, representing the European Union at an Ad Hoc Working Group on the Causes of Conflict and the Promotion of Peace and Sustainable Development in Africa.[13] "It is a precondition," he continued, "to the success of democracy and good governance, and it is crucial to progress in other related fields, such as health, gender equity and social welfare.... However, in many African countries, economic and demographic trends have seriously undermined education systems. The educational sector," he bleakly but correctly stated, "continues to be severely underfunded in the national budgets and the trend towards providing universal primary education has, in many cases, been reversed....In some countries, the number of newly graduated teachers is lower than the number of teachers dying from HIV/AIDS."[14]

In light of this shocking pronouncement, the very idea that some African nations hold up beacons not simply for the continent, but for the world, cannot be emphasized enough. In fact, an ironic statistical analysis shows that despite the tremendous setbacks, African nations as a whole spend a proportionally larger percentage of their budgets on education than any other region of the world and one of the lowest proportional percentages on military defense.[15]

This study, divided into three basic sections, seeks to briefly examine secondary school education in two such African nations, to look at these systems vis-à-vis New York-based alternative schools, and to devise some practical work that U.S. educators may use in their day-to-day adventures. The first section, "Educational Apartheid: Education under Fire," sets the context. Pre-independence education in Eritrea and education in South Africa before the first democratic elections of 1994 are described. Education in the U.S. both prior to the civil rights era and in the "postmulticultural" present is also looked at, as are the current effects of globalization on educational endeavors throughout the African continent.

The second and primary section of this volume looks at the modern-day search for educational alternatives. Beginning with a global Pan-Africanist perspective, this section chronicles national and local projects of South Africa, Eritrea, and several different specific examples within New York's alternative, adult, and continuing education schools and programs. The final section, "Learning from Africa: Teaching about Human Rights in the U.S.," draws conclusions from the comparisons and includes some hands-on suggestions for social and educational change.

One South African National Report, "Preparing for the 21st Century Through Education, Training and Work," suggests that the pressure for "flexible learning" modalities will be a "major catalyst" across the many fields of international educational reform. All education providers, the report authors write, "should take advantage of new information and communication technologies to support flexible delivery."[16] While this writer has always supported a flexible and pragmatic approach — calling on administrators, teachers, and students to be strategic and think critically before taking action for educational equity and social justice — now is an especially important time to make a distinction between simple flexibility and one's basic principles. This is a moment for reflection and renewal, across national boundaries and across our own racial and social divides. It is a matter of some urgency to take serious stock, in this calm before the coming storms.

SECTION I

EDUCATIONAL APARTHEID: EDUCATION UNDER FIRE

Chapter 1

"OUTSIDERS" — CONTEMPORARY EDUCATION IN THE U.S.

Though controversial in their sweeping overviews and undeniably mainstream pronouncements, the research and writings of George Fredrickson are fundamental to any cross-cultural study of the U.S. and South Africa. Fredrickson's influential *White Supremacy: A Comparative Study in American and South African History* (1981) made a decisive contribution to the study of these two dissimilar yet connected countries. Carefully defining white supremacy as a series of attitudes, ideologies, and policies associated with blatant forms of white or European dominance over nonwhite populations, Fredrickson maintains that the term is designed to be distinct from simple forms of prejudice and discrimination. These last concepts, he suggests, are common to all multiracial societies, whereas white supremacy is characterized by its systematic and self-conscious efforts "to make race or color a qualification for membership in the civil community." South Africa and the United States, Fredrickson asserts, stand out in their development of race distinction. "The term 'white supremacy' applies with particular force to the historical experience" of these two nations.[1]

Obvious comparisons may be made between South Africa's recent modern-day apartheid and the U.S. South's era of slavery and segregation, yet Fredrickson begins by looking beyond those two stark periods. More than any other multiracial society, he notes, the U.S. and South Africa have developed "over long periods of time a tendency to push the principle of differentiation by race to its logical outcome" — a society in which non-Europeans, whatever their class or cultural or economic status, are treated in some respects as a grouping, in a manner suggesting permanent alienation, outsider status, and the burden of "otherness." Beyond simply offering comparative antiracist perspectives, Frederickson's approach as a historian is valuable for its ability to, in his words, "escape the provincialism and limiting set of tacit assumptions that tend to result from perpetual immersion in the study of a single culture, a preoccupation that is especially constricting if that culture happens to be our own."[2]

The peculiarities I've faced as a student of African history and a teacher of both high school social studies and multicultural education for staff members have led me to great sympathy with the ideals put forth in the comparative historical study of *White Supremacy*. One striking "translation," written to evoke a U.S. consciousness around the need for critical comparison, suggests a "what if" scenario regarding the Native American/American Indian nations. We are asked to imagine an early U.S. society where indigenous peoples were not substantially decimated and where European colonial and immigrant populations were smaller in numbers than was, in fact, the historical case. Once the whites seize, as they did, the most arable lands with most exploitable resources and once the Indians are, as they were, consigned to confined, less farmable areas (in this imaginary case, simply a greatly enlarged version of the still-existing reservation system), all that needs to take place is a division of citizenship rights and a few "Jim Crow"-type laws. That individual Native nations would be used against one another in a divide-and-conquer strategy is, itself, a matter of historical fact, not imagination. This "not inconceivable scenario," writes Frederickson, "is useful not merely to make the essential features of apartheid explicable to Americans, but also to help deflate any notion that white Americans have a kind of 'innate moral superiority over white South Africans.'"[3] There is, indeed, much to suggest that the architects of apartheid studied the U.S. system of Native reservations in setting up their policies for South African townships.

Regarding educational policy, the ultimate implications of the segregationist Jim Crow philosophy, which had an effect on the entire nation, are summarized by Frederickson's quote of prominent southern educator Thomas Pierce Bailey: "Let the lowest white man count more than the highest negro."[4] Though much has been written detailing education for African Americans from the 1910s to the present,[5] a noteworthy factor in *White Supremacy*'s description is the contextual parallels especially in this field. "The comparable educational trends that occurred around the turn of the century in the Cape (South Africa's Cape Town was and is home to the majority of the 'colored' — neither African nor European — of that country's many racial castes) and the South," comments Frederickson, "both involved successful campaigns for school reform that ended up benefiting whites only."[6] This interesting footnote, often overlooked, provides some clues as to what may have been in those days a more subtle maneuver toward racism than many would have liked to admit. Segregation in the U.S. certainly existed well before 1900 and the Jim Crow developments, but inferior education — characterized by the public school systems nationally — included large numbers of poor whites as well as the entire African (American) population. The progressive reformers of the public school movements of the early twentieth century upgraded white schools while reducing funding for Black education.[7] The drive toward compulsory education in this period was applied only toward whites. The mixture of race and class oppression, more complicated in the days of Reconstruction following the end of the Civil War and as early as "emancipation," was simplified on this point in the manner suggested by Bailey; the formation of a permanent Black racial underclass intensified as slavery was formally abolished.

Frederickson forcefully argues that twentieth-century education in South Africa as well as in the U.S. served primarily to limit economic, political, and social positions of people of African descent and to subordinate them. "The two patterns of educational discrimination arose out of analogous circumstances," he asserts, "and provided equivalent advantages for the white community."[8] Cheap and menial agricultural workers were needed in both countries, and whole families — including school-age children — were to be used in these endeavors as a perpetually "unskilled" labor pool. This economic incentive, however, does not explain the philosophical underpinnings and political implications of increased and upgraded education for poor whites. "In part," Frederickson aptly explains, "this impulse was due to the upsurge of ideological racism." The "burden of ethnic hegemony," at a time when all whites were needed on "the front lines of imperial consolidation or on the watch towers of 'racial purity,'"[9] meant that education systems had to reflect distinguishable inequalities. Even as the policies of the early twentieth century gave way to upsurges at the middle and end of the century, and as revolutionary tumult in Africa saw to an end of the colonial era and ultimate dismantling of legal apartheid, it is hard to say that the imperial aspirations of most U.S. governmental figures have in any way diminished.

The conclusion of *White Supremacy* suggests that the comparison of the post-civil rights era in the U.S. with South Africa before the end of apartheid is difficult at best. Nevertheless, Frederickson admits that the persistence of de facto segregation in contemporary U.S. society, "particularly in the allocation of urban space and in education," makes it clear that the elimination of the Jim Crow laws in no way guaranteed "equality and fraternity" among those historically disenfranchised.[10] For educators especially it is daunting to understand the depth of our own profession's role in this long and deep process of oppression.

Sonia Nieto, professor of language, literacy, and culture at the University of Massachusetts, Amherst, School of Education — herself a teacher who "worked her way up" through the New York City school system — has made many contributions in light of this larger task, chronicling the crisis of contemporary education in the U.S. and positing some straightforward solutions in the name of affirming diversity. In "A Gesture Toward Justice," Nieto summarized some of the best modern research in noting: "Major problems facing urban public schools include lack of resources (Kozol, 1991), inadequate preparation of teachers (Darling-Hammond, 1998), policies and practices that discourage engagement with learning (Nieto, 1999), and racism and other biases that reflect deeply seated structural inequalities in society (Lipman, 1998)."[11] As the urban public school has itself become a metaphor for the education primarily of students of color, this listing is all the more damning. Insofar as these issues continue to affect specialized, community-based spaces, such as

New York's alternative high schools and programs, Nieto goes on to express that "small schools by themselves can do little to change these conditions." They are not, for example, inherently antiracist, and one cited report (Jervis, 1996) finds that in a new school "most teachers conspicuously avoided issues of race and difference, despite their expressed commitment to structures that supported equity and respected diversity."[12]

Far from a harsh critic of the small schools movement, Nieto is still careful to view any educational reform effort in the greater context of social change and social justice. She discusses a study with which she was personally involved concerning high school dropouts among Puerto Rican youth of one U.S. town. The "scandalous" figure of a 68 percent dropout rate was compounded by the interviews with some of those who had left school. One noted, "I felt alone"; another, "I was an outsider." In this context, Nieto writes that "small schools can be an antidote to an educational system that has lost its soul as it has become more bureaucratic and impersonal."[13] But these schools must not simply be small or community centered; they must redefine the process of teaching and learning to turn the practices of white supremacy and injustice on their heads.

An important challenge that attempts to put current U.S. educational practices into an appropriate historical context was recently issued by the political edition of the e-column "Seeing Black." Makani Themba-Nixon's "School 'Choice' and Other White Lies" addresses both a private and a public assessment of the public school system and the growing call for vouchers. In it, she recounts her harrowing experiences as a six-year-old girl in 1966, one of six Black children "integrating" an all-white school in Queens through the busing experiments of that era. She notes the "fascinating transition" from the time one century ago when conservative forces were attempting to make public schools mandatory in order to teach the "American way of life" to immigrants and others who might hold on to "foreign values." Identifying the Ku Klux Klan as a major advocate of these attendance laws, Themba-Nixon suggests that today truly integrated public schools pose a threat to a narrow Eurocentric Americanism.[14]

Tracing "the roots" of Black-white inequality, Themba-Nixon reminds readers that emancipated men and women were promised access to education (then termed "the great equalizer"), but that both during slavery and in the postslavery period, the "loaning" of "indentured" children of African descent for service as apprentices in exchange for school tuition financing of the children of white "owners" was common. The obvious conclusion regarding schooling today is that "the debt concerning education is a literal one."[15] Not surprisingly, calls within the Black community for fiscal and political reparations continue to grow, as dramatically demonstrated at the August 2001 United Nations World Conference on the Elimination of Racism, held in Durban, South Africa.[16]

The crux of the debate around school vouchers and the role of public education centers around a switch in focus from "unteachable" students to "dysfunctional" schools. Themba-Nixon reviews right wing-funded television ads of the Black Alliance for Education Options (BAEO), which suggest that school "choice" and vouchers (rather than well-trained teachers or better-than-adequate resources) are the true rescuers of the cause of Black education. For her, the BAEO takes a disturbing shift away from community accountability. That conservatives are taking a strong interest in Black schooling is noteworthy; that taxpayers under these auspices are no longer seen as a community unit committed to education for all is "the ultimate breach in the social contract." Themba-Nixon correctly relates the unfinished agenda of the early civil rights movement with the educational challenges faced today. "Many Black people put their lives on the line in the fight for quality education for all," she concludes. "This was the real choice movement."[17]

Urban school systems have fewer choices to offer any student today, as the fairness of school funding comes into question, revealing the true lack of priority given to education throughout the U.S. By the end of 2002, nineteen states had had their school funding process deemed unconstitutional by state courts. New York State, in many ways representative of the extremes of this problem, was rendered an embarrassing decision in a landmark case brought about by the Campaign for Fiscal Equity (CFE).

When an appellate court stated, in the now infamous DeGrasse case, that educational opportunity was only guaranteed through the eighth grade, shock waves were sent throughout the national school reform movement. By the summer of 2003, however, the New York State Court of Appeals unequivocally reversed, almost in its entirety, the lower court's findings. The Court of Appeals clearly stated that a "meaningful high school education" must be provided for all citizens according to the state constitution. Citing the need for smaller class sizes and appropriate computer technology in all schools, the highest court in the state required the legislature to ascertain the actual cost of a sound, basic education — especially in underfunded New York City — to ensure that every school had necessary resources, and to ensure that a system of accountability be set up. With a one-year deadline for implementing necessary reforms by late 2004, this decision marked a "powerful remedy," according to the CFE, for past injustices. "No other U.S. state court," the CFE noted, "has decisively rejected" minimal middle school-level literacy and calculating skills.[18]

Language issues have been and are also pervasive in the set of problems facing U.S. education. The case of the New York school district where bilingual students were, at one moment, labeled as learning disabled because of minor lags in their English writing ability, then quickly relabeled after successful court suits as gifted because of their unique fluency in two languages, is now the stuff of legend. The work of community organizations like ASPIRA, Inc., in fighting for these reforms is notable. "La Lucha Continua" is a fact that almost needs no further comment. In addition to Nieto's research, countless studies and anecdotes throughout the country document a series of misunderstood policies regarding dual language instruction. Mexican American principal Tamara Witzl, who helped design a small, neighborhood alternative school in the center of Chicago's "Little Village," puts it this way in a conversation with writer Gabrielle Lyon: "The connection between language, culture, family and community is a direct link. When you take away people's ability to communicate with their parents, uncles, grandparents, you break down a very human element — for that individual, as well as in communities and society as a whole."[19]

A stark challenge to George W. Bush's No Child Left Behind Act, regarding language and family, was brought up late in 2005 at a summit of the National Congress of American Indians (by no means a radical group). Citing cuts of thousands of teachers throughout rural areas of the U.S., the Native leaders reported that the Act was directly responsible for making it difficult to recruit and retain qualified educators. Lillian Sparks, the executive director of the National Indian Education Association, stated that "culture and language were not being considered" by the Bush administration's directives.[20] An even more damning indictment was made by author Jonathan Kozol, whose book *The Shame of the Nation: The Restoration of Apartheid Schooling in America* was published in 2005 to much media fanfare. Noting that "segregation has returned to public education with a vengeance," [21] Kozol argues that the crisis of modern American schooling is that separate is still unequal.

Finally, the state of U.S. schools and society can be no better summarized than by Deborah Meier, founder of the Center for Collaborative Education and leader in New York's alternative schools movement through the Central Park East initiatives. In her essay "The Crisis of Relationships," Meier suggests that one root of the problem of education today is that "the glue that holds responsible relationships with other people together has largely disappeared. We do not belong," she continues, "to anywhere near as many stable communities — workplaces, hometowns, neighborhoods, or extended families — as we once did." In this disintegration of social and family life, the effect on education has been particularly devastating, with the model of the large-scale, industrial-size and -styled school irreparably outdated and rife with all the injustices of the past century of inequality. Meier is succinct: "Public schools have lost their public."[22]

The U.S. today has no slavery, no overt segregation or apartheid laws, much commentary on racism and sexism, and an African American on the Supreme Court and in the office of secretary of state. But when one looks carefully and critically at the conditions of education for Black (or non-European) America, a single thread of history can be drawn at least one hundred years back. Rev. Martin Luther King Jr., in his all-too-quoted "I Have a Dream" speech, spoke of marching on Washington, D.C., in an effort to cash in an uncollected check. Few of his followers would argue that those funds — at the very least in regard to education — remain "past due," with no interest accumulated. The building of alternative schools and institutions must be done with these facts in mind. Good intentions and minor reforms will not be enough to raise student standards and lower educators' tolerance for sometimes subtle injustices. It is time to look at schools that have faced radical transformations — to learn what lessons may lead us out of an all-too-commonplace elitism.

Chapter 2

WE HAVE OUR VOICES:
ERITREA IN THE PRE-INDEPENDENCE ERA

The fundamental irony of education in Eritrea, the Horn of Africa country that fought against numerous colonial contenders, is that the period during the fight for independence — as much as anything that has taken place since full political freedom was achieved — characterizes the country's extraordinary and inspiring efforts in the areas of literacy promotion, respect for diverse cultures, advancement of multilingualism, and promotion of gender equality. Remarkably, a nation forced and fortified to endure a thirty-year war against neighboring Ethiopia — backed at one period by the United States and at another by the Soviet Union, leaving Eritrea caught in the middle of cold war controversies — developed both education as a priority and educational innovations as a matter of course. Eritrea's unusual history makes it unique and not necessarily a model, but its attempts at transformation are too compelling and important for educators internationally to deny its careful study.

A synopsis of Eritrea's colonial period indicates Italy's benign neglect, similar to its control of the nearby (not neighboring) African colonies of Libya and Somalia. Education was mostly handled by Protestant and Roman Catholic missionaries; instruction was in Italian and concentrated on menial agricultural skills, assorted military functions, and "hygiene" — meant to reduce the dangers of contamination (perhaps of Africanism?) to the small Italian population.[1] During the fascist period of Italy's history, instruction became increasingly strict and limited: fourth grade was the highest allowable level of achievement, and schooling in general was not encouraged. In 1941, when the tide was turning in the Allied fight against Italian fascism, a British

Military Administration (BMA) was installed to oversee Eritrea. The British felt that they had, in light of the Italians' neglect, inherited a "huge task," and they set out in their civilizing mission of English colonization to train an Eritrean elite group of interpreters, clerks, and paraprofessionals.[2]

Though the British undoubtedly multiplied the number of primary schools and expanded the curriculum taught, education was still focused in a Eurocentric context. Perhaps the most significant positive contribution of the eleven-year BMA period was the development of texts not simply in English and Arabic (from the roughly 50 percent of the population that was and is Muslim), but also in the language of a majority of Eritreans, Tigrinya. Teacher training was encouraged in a trilingual format, and the Eritrean thirst for education was somewhat sated.

The peculiarities of the history of the Horn of Africa are rarely clearer than when reviewing the early 1950s, as Eritrea was passed for ten years to a "federation" with Ethiopia. During the scramble for Africa, the Ethiopian monarchs shrewdly bargained with Italy (in part using Eritrea as a buffer and item of trade) to maintain its own independence — making it one of the only African nations to remain free of European colonialism. Once a peace treaty was signed at the end of World War II, Libya and Somalia were ultimtely granted independence by the Allies, leaving the fate of Eritrea to an indecisive and weak United Nations. Ethiopia's emperor of that period, the passionate Haile Selassie, argued that a union with his country would create a stronger and more stable area. Despite Ethiopian bombings and assassinations of Eritrean independentists, the UN General Assembly adopted this idea, with U.S. Secretary of State John Foster Dulles succinctly stating that "from the point of view of justice, the opinions of the Eritrean people must receive consideration. Nevertheless," he continued, "the strategic interest of the U.S. in the Red Sea basin and considerations of security and world peace make it necessary that the country has to be linked with our ally, Ethiopia."[3] Thus was set into motion a period that resulted in Africa's longest continuous war, at the cost of an incredible amount of material resources, not to mention number of lives.

Education under the federated union followed a pattern set up regarding most of Eritrea's social, political, and educational life: it was dominated by Ethiopian officials. In 1956, Amharic, the official language of Ethiopia, was proclaimed the only language to be used for schools and public offices, and by the end of the decade thousands of students were jailed for participating in campaigns against repressive Ethiopian academic policies. Economic life was shut down, newspapers were censored, the Eritrean flag was banned; finally, in 1962, Emperor Selassie terminated the federation, annexing Eritrea into the Ethiopian state. Eritrea's borders had been literally erased from the maps of the world, and Selassie — who greatly influenced the then newly created Organization of African Unity — presided over the decision that the then-current (in most cases, colonial) borders be maintained, as any alternative notion would be too confusing. Following annexation, Arabic and Tigrinya textbooks were burned, enrollment in schools was frozen despite an outcry for expanded education, and the newly developed Eritrean liberation movements began an all-out war for independence in response to the intensifying decimation of their country.[4]

By 1974, the war — politically and economically costly for the Western-backed Ethiopians — combined with internal corruption and incompetence to bring about an overthrow of Selassie and the traditional Coptic monarchy in favor of a military regime. The Dergue military government, denied arms and aid by a now-cautious West, turned to the Soviet Union and received more than $2 billion worth of mainly military support in a very short time. The socialist-oriented Eritrean People's Liberation Front (EPLF), having won significant support among the Eritrean people in a drive for Christian-Muslim unity, may have hoped for an opening toward independence, but the Dergue and the Soviet Union saw Eritrea's Red Sea ports as too strategically important to give up. In 1978, a force of over 100,000 Ethiopian troops pushed into Eritrea to crush the movement. In the words of Dan Connell, a prominent U.S. historian of Eritrean affairs, the EPLF and other freedom fighters were not destroyed, as expected, but did have to withdraw into a "phase of extreme isolation, as the Soviet-led political embargo took effect and the West simply walked away."[5] Needless to say, schooling under the Dergue saw a new round of intensified repression, as educated Eritreans became a particular target for harassment and torture, including the detention and murder of thousands of students.

As the 1980s brought widespread famine to the entire region, with Ethiopia particularly hard hit, the EPLF began to rebuild its base with a focus on self-reliance and a special emphasis on education in liberated zones of the country. In the Sahel Province, long a base of EPLF support, a Zero School was established — so named because the movement was starting with no resources — that ultimately developed into a laboratory for change and the center of a 1983-87 national literacy campaign.

The work of the Zero or Revolution School and the literacy campaign is aptly chronicled in Les Gottesman's *To Fight and Learn: The Praxis and Promise of Literacy in Eritrea's Independence War* (1998). "In and through education," Gottesman observes, "Eritreans have reflected on issues of power and leadership, culture and national identity, and tradition and social change." Communities, he asserts, have acted decisively and unequivocally to support their own liberation in both individual and collective ways — using education and literacy as their chief mechanism for change. They have "used education to envision their future, to dream responsibly what they will become in a country 'beyond war'...free of colonialism, drought, famine, and ignorance. Education, they insist, greater than hope, is both a promise and a warrant of the future they have acted to secure."[6]

"Illiteracy is our main enemy" was among the first slogans of the EPLF, recalled Saleh Mahmud, an early student in the Zero School and teacher during the literacy campaign. First, the Front ran literacy campaigns for its own fighters, achieving the goal of 100 percent literacy among the EPLF as early as 1972. By the 1980s, all new recruits who had less than seven years of schooling completed their education within the Front's schools. A highly motivated and informed fighting force, it was argued, would be more effective than a passive one simply responding to orders.[7] At the Zero School, all the teachers and students learned together, worked together, and lived together, with the lines between teacher and student blurred as they struggled cooperatively, all fighters.[8]

Ayn Alem Marcos, a leader of the Asmara Teachers Training Institute, described the 1983 "dispatch" of over 450 Zero School students throughout the country, "behind enemy lines," to begin the campaign process for universal literacy. "The rationale behind this dispatch," Marcos explained, "was to give the students firsthand experience of being integrated in the community, and also for them to conduct a pilot study in the eradication of illiteracy from society."[9] By 1987, the campaign reached 56,000 adults, 60 percent of them women — an astounding number given the historic reticence about having girls receive schooling. In describing how teacher-fighters went back and forth from community to Front, in communication with the movement's leadership but also in constant contact with the local people in any given area, Marcos noted that "we happened to design a curriculum and produce materials for reading, writing and numeration."[10] In most cases, this placed teachers at particular risk, with schools accessible to the people but close to enemy camps. Commenting on the literacy campaign process, Gottesman highlights this point as "a dialectic within the EPLF's practice; a creative tension between study and planning on the one hand, and on-the-spot experimentation, the use of observation and dialogue, learning by doing on the other hand."[11] In this way, education changed the communities and the communities changed education — all within the context of the liberation movement itself.

In fact, by the time of liberation in 1991 and 1993, many of the more experienced (and therefore more educated) of the fighter-teachers had been killed in the war. A key issue identified for postindependence Eritrea was teacher training; after an "exemplary" tradition in the field, the Front was faced with an urgent need to reintegrate the remaining and younger fighters into society.[12] But an ethos had been established of the connection between literacy as both a basic human right and a contributor toward human needs. The EPLF recognized, according to Lionel Cliffe, African studies professor at Leeds University, that "different patterns of mobilization are required in different regions" — with literacy fundamental to these mobilizations.

The principle that each region's language, culture, and desires would be recognized in the larger national agenda had become embedded in EPLF practice.

Much of this belief is represented by the Eritrean commitment to multilingualism, accepting nine official languages as part of their postindependence program. Tesfamicael Gerahto, head of the Curriculum Development Institute, stated that "if the mother tongue is used educating in a certain nationality, what you are actually doing is, you're trying to develop the pride, nationality pride, of the community." In this way, people can be "motivated and interested to promote their culture, to participate equally in the nation's overall reconstruction strategies," and to play a part in "the national unity of the country."[13] In questioning this "unity in diversity" model, Gottesman asks: "If a community wanted a language other than the mother tongue, would there be something that would be worth discussing?"[14] The reply — that parents' committees, people's councils, and the community at large would go through a process of consultation as to why they might want another language (say, Arabic for religious reasons or English because it is an international language) — speaks volumes regarding the intentions of a dialogical process. The national leadership, for their part, would explain their rationale for an emphasis on primary language development.

The end of the official EPLF national literacy campaign in 1987 also corresponded with a heightening of strategic military offensives, taking control of more towns and villages. Ultimately, in March of 1988, in an original move contrary to all basic precepts of people's war, the EPLF struck at the strongest Ethiopian garrisons, playing into a demoralization that had set in for the Addis Ababa regime regarding what seemed like an unending struggle. Over the following year, the EPLF was able to substantially expand their armed forces, and by May of 1991, they retook control of their own capital city of Asmara, thereby ending the thirty-year war. They set up a provisional government lasting until May of 1993, when an internationally monitored referendum officially pronounced the will of the Eritrean people: 99.8 percent of them voted for full and complete independence. The promise and hopes of independence were understandably high, most particularly in the much-lauded field of education. Scholar Roy Pateman, in his revised *Eritrea: Even the Stars Are Burning* (1998), noted that 80 percent of the male and 90 percent of the female population were still illiterate at the time of liberation. Though education supplied to EPLF members through the Revolution School network far outweighed surrounding systems (i.e., a fifth grade Zero School education was reported to be equivalent to a twelfth grade education in Ethiopia), the need for a truly national curriculum revision was pressing. Beraki Gebreselassie, director of the Zero School who became Eritrea's first minister of education, noted to Pateman that one of Eritrea's chief postliberation priorities had to be "integration of the curriculum."[15]

In his extensive conversations with Les Gottesman, Gebreselassie notes that the situation immediately following liberation was in some ways "very conducive" to running schools, given that most of the educational innovations carried out by the EPLF in the 1980s were done in the midst of war. "It was very difficult to run schools very easily because there were aerial bombardments," he states. "So we in fact were forced to run schools at night, in caves."[16]

An early report of the Provisional Government's Department of Education (converted to a ministry following the May 1993 referendum) cited problems that included an unequal distribution of educational opportunities; a big shortage of schools and a large number of schools badly damaged; a severe shortage of school materials and equipment; a shortage of teachers, both in quantity and in qualifications; a very low academic level among students; an acute shortage of technicians, technical students, and technical know-how; a high illiteracy rate; and a depressed state of Eritrean culture among the nine ethnic groups of the country — due to the decades-long imposition of Amharic language and culture.[17]

Still, many Eritrean intellectuals were hopeful, given the emphasis and history of the liberation movement and the mass mobilization of the population over a long period. Harvard-educated Eritrean scholar and professor Asmarom Legasse noted that, as the EPLF spent most of its "career" amidst the majority farming population of the country, the Front began governance with an "intimate familiarity with the rural population to a much greater extent than is true of other parts of Africa."[18] When asked about the potential bureaucratization of the EPLF once in power, Eritrean president Isaias Afwerki commented, "We're going to be empirical.…Our only criterion for a policy is whether it works for the people. Nothing's carved in stone. I hope we've learned that much from the mistakes of other revolutions."[19]

Without a doubt, few liberation movements have had the practical hurdles and humanistic responses so integral to the Eritrean experience. That this unity across religious lines and ethnic divides was a major raison d'être for the very founding of the EPLF, later articulated in their language policies, sets them apart. That education of women and girls was made a priority early in their struggle was uncommon. That a pedagogy within the movement developed, centering around the concept of teacher-as-learner and student-as-teacher, with complete integration into local communities of often different ethnicity than the teachers, was unprecedented. The Eritrean liberation movement, more than most anticolonial struggles one can think of, was based on precepts of progressive education — giving voice to the interests of the common person. As internationally recognized Eritrean poet Reeson Haile wrote, scribed in his native Tigrinya, "We have our voice." The challenge now was to multiply those voices calling out, creating a chorus that would include the entire population.

Chapter 3

TIME IS TIGHT: EDUCATION IN SOUTH AFRICA UNDER APARTHEID

With a wealth of printed material written about education during South Africa's apartheid years, it is easy to get a clear picture of the nature of its inequities. The diversity of perspectives, however, sometimes clouds the basic issues, with approaches ranging from descriptive (Kallaway, 1984; Unterhalter, Wolpe, and Botha, 1992) to radical (Alexander, 1992), from Western-focused (Marcum, 1982) to Africanist with an educational liberation bent (Nkomo, 1990). There are also within this field a number of volumes that discuss reform and alternatives attempted within the apartheid system, from personal (de Villiers, 1990) to community church-based (Christie, 1998) to African student-oriented (Open School, 1987). An important conference on "Education for Affirmation," which took place during the height of the South African resistance movements of the 1980s, is also chronicled and reported upon (SACC, 1988).[1]

The purpose of this chapter is not to delve too deeply into the world of discrimination that characterized education under apartheid, but to give a brief review of the basic origins of apartheid's educational systems, as well to look at some of the more innovative reforms. The former objective has already been adequately summarized by Ken Hartshorne. Hartshorne worked first in South Africa's missionary schools of the 1940s before becoming a critical inspector and planner within the Bantu Education Departments of the 1950s and '60s. Shifting politics, as so many did following the pivotal 1976 Soweto student uprising against Bantu education, he then resigned his position, ultimately becoming a leading member of the De Lange Commission of 1980 — a group that attempted to look beyond the divisiveness of then-current apartheid policies.[2] As he wrote in the days following the fall of apartheid, "because of their very nature and function, schools and the education system in general" — referring especially to South Africa in the 1950s through '80s, but also to a broader critique — "are open to divisions, dissent, and protest in society. If the authority of the state is questioned at any level, this will be reflected in the school as surely as the school itself also in essence reflects the values of the state that controls it."[3]

Associating schools everywhere as "sites of struggle" and "centers of resistance," Hartshorne recounted the 1948 founding of the separate development policies of Christian National Education for whites and Bantu Education for Blacks. The leaders of the Institute for Christian National Education, initially setting up a blueprint for Afrikaans-speaking schooling, also suggested (in theory) that native Africans would be "helped along" culturally by separate and unequal systems. English-speaking whites, in fact, were included in the finer schools, though the "Boer nation" gave themselves sole responsibility for "senior trusteeship" over the "backward" Africans.[4]

By the early 1950s, the draconian Boer worldview of precise racial typecasting led to unprecedented fragmentation through a national education system with nineteen separate and distinct structures. A hierarchy was created leaving all structures in the "nonwhite" communities with a proportionally tiny percentage of financing, resources, and facilities. By the end of the 1960s, these conditions were coupled with a tightly consolidated central government, which used repression and force when mere civil controls were no longer tolerated. Though violence and massacre, as was used in Sharpeville against unarmed protestors, had some temporarily quieting effects, the building of tensions — termed "inevitable" by Hartshorne and other far-from-progressive onlookers — led to the 1976 explosion of student protest in South Africa's largest Black township, Soweto. The Soweto uprising centered around issues of language and the idea that while dominant majority African languages such as KwaZulu and Xhosa were effectively banned in the schools, the "new" white language of Afrikaans — recognized nowhere outside of the small community of South African Boers — was mandatory for all. So-called "Bantu" schools were boycotted and shut down, with growing support of parents and teachers. By 1980, the complete breakdown of education among the majority of the country's people led the government's Human Sciences Research Council to convene the De Lange Commission, charged with investigating the state of education in the divided nation.[5]

The commission, though a quasi-official government body, came up with surprisingly progressive recommendations. A two-year process of what Hartshorne termed "dilution" led to a more palatable government white paper that resulted in sweeping 1984 legislative measures designed principally to change the face of apartheid while keeping the fundamental racist project intact. A key De Lange principle, for example, was that "education shall give positive recognition to the freedom of choice of the individual, parents and organizations in society." The 1984 white paper maintained that principle, but added that it would be "subject to the provisions of any law regarding the attending of a school for a particular population group by a pupil of another population group." At this point, the main law in question — the Christian National Education and Policy Acts — was unequivocally upheld by the apartheid regime.[6]

The "investigations" of De Lange and other official reform measures — in the educational field, among others — were merely backdrop for the larger constitutional struggle of the moment. After banning all major liberation groups and parties in the 1960s, and using widespread jailings, disappearances, and assassinations in the 1970s, the racist regime put forth the idea of a Tricameral Parliament, whereby Indians and "coloreds" could vote — but in separate and subservient assembly halls. Reaction to the tricameral proposal was swift and decisive: a new resistance movement was born that would not dwindle until the final end of complete apartheid ten years later. The United Democratic Front (UDF), bringing together a huge coalition of community groups for an atypically outspoken series of protests (given the level of prior repression), was formed to fight for freedom, equality, and a widespread boycott of tricameralism.

Ultimately, South African Defense Force troops were sent into the townships to keep order in a society that was becoming increasingly ungovernable. A larger-than-ever grouping of whites began to see the need to take an anti-apartheid position; a Mass Democratic Movement was created that by 1990 had unstoppable momentum. Once Nelson Mandela and dozens of other long-term political prisoners were freed, the African National Congress (ANC), Pan Africanist Congress (PAC), South African Communist Party, and other liberation groups were unbanned. Negotiations led to a "one person, one vote" universal election, and in 1994 millions turned out in a peaceful show of determination; Mandela was elected president and the ANC held a huge majority in a multiparty Parliament.

During the height of the anti-apartheid movements of the 1980s, two inspiring, alternative projects symbolized the visions of those educational professionals committed to justice. Inside the country, the South African Council of Churches (SACC) — a longstanding nongovernmental grouping with a strong anti-apartheid position — remained unbanned because of their historic Christian representation. As a founding participant in the UDF, the SACC also helped put together the National Education Crisis Committee and various conferences of families and friends of those jailed without charge, the detainees. In 1987, a number of these forces joined with the South African Committee for Higher Education (SACHED) and created the EWE study program: Each Working in Education. In addition to its value as an acronym, linking to the concept of everyone playing a role of teacher — "each one, teach one" — *ewe* is also the Xhosa word for "yes." The resistance movements were ready to assert their positive ideas, no longer satisfied with boycotts against the corrupt system. Even before the end of apartheid, some communities began to rebuild.[7]

The EWE study program began as a correspondence course, with detainees communicating with one another and with educators from SACHED and from their townships of origin. Writing from their jail cells, the prisoners helped develop a concept of alternative education that encompassed content, method, and practice. "We believe," the detainees wrote, "that the only practice that is just and viable is a democratic one, where one recognizes fully every person's right to participate and create...where one recognizes that people have experience and they have a role to play in education. We want to show," they summarized, echoing other struggles we've surveyed, "that learners can teach and teachers can learn."[8]

The foundation of the EWE study program was based on what the participants termed "immovable facts" and "firm beliefs." They understood as given that they were living under repressive conditions, with no formal teachers available within the prisons and with only government-determined syllabuses and textbooks outside of prison in the impoverished townships. Their first two beliefs, already common within the framework of education for liberation, were that learning should lead to empowerment through democracy and that each individual had something they could and should teach another. Their second two beliefs deserve closer notation, as they are somewhat less common in the progressive lexicon of ideas. "Unified and disciplined action," they wrote, "is a key to success."[9] The focus on discipline, more associated with armed struggle or with autocratic pedagogy than with "open schooling" and popular reforms, signified the seriousness of the EWE grouping. They clearly viewed themselves as leaders in the struggle against apartheid much more than as victims of its repressive apparatus. That their jargon matched the rhetoric of the then-banned ANC was surely no coincidence.

"Methods of learning," they continued, "are more important than the content of learning."[10] Here, EWE diverges slightly from the more typical progressive doctrines, which certainly acknowledge the importance of both methodology and curriculum, but are not usually as willing to elevate method above the syllabus to be taught. One must wonder whether this hierarchy of importance was, in part, based on the many decades in South Africa where no content was close to relevant for the African majority. One must simultaneously question whether a reliance on content is not based largely on the driven need in contemporary U.S. society to "increase standards" or have students be able to "compete" with their European counterparts.

In any case, the EWE project affected both prisoners and community-based educators, leading to an enhanced surge of energy and sense of possibility — at least in the Eastern Cape where it was initiated. Though careful to state that each region of the country would have to design its own alternatives appropriate to its own needs, EWE clearly demonstrated to all teachers and students of education that an inspiring pedagogy was possible, even within the most repressive, racist contexts.

Outside of South Africa during roughly the same period, a school was being built for those fighters in exile. The Solomon Mahlango Freedom College (SOMAFCO), run by the ANC in East African Tanzania, was founded in 1977 for a new generation of activists who fled the country following the clampdown after the Soweto uprising. With thousands of students — some as young as six — jailed after the uprising for a typical six-month period, thousands more were flocking to Tanzania and the ANC camps that were operating there. Though facilities from preschool to postgraduate were needed, a secondary school was built first, named after a 22-year-old teacher-in-training who had left the field to join the ANC and was subsequently executed by the apartheid state.[11]

Though stress, fear, and uncertainty were part of the daily routine at this part-educational/part-military exile camp, SOMAFCO became a haven of international renown, dedicated to education and literacy for all — with a special emphasis on the writing of one's personal history through poetry. Though English was the common language of communication and instruction, students were not discouraged from writing in their native tongue, and a racial and ethnic mixture among the students and teachers was the norm. Ultimately, a primary school was established, with student work of all generations meticulously collected and preserved as a testimony to the liberation struggle.[12]

The EWE and SOMAFCO examples are symbolic of the possibilities so ripe in the South African movements of the 1980s and early '90s. How "disappointment" and "disillusionment" could become catchwords of the educational field following the fall of apartheid seems difficult to believe. Hartshorne, who played a minor role early in the transitional period after

1994, discussed government policy as a "discourse of good intentions,"[13] with the harsh realities of the past and huge, continuing economic inequities preventing a fast enough change following the euphoria of the election of Mandela. In the first year of democratic governance, education was given the largest share of government expenditure (23 percent of the national budget), but this was drastically cut in the following two years.[14]

Many have tried to account for the shifts in policy and priority. Linda Chisolm, in an article on the restructuring of South African education and training, suggests that the world context needs to be examined. "A fundamental impetus to the reform of education," she writes, "has come from the perceived link between education, economic growth and international competitiveness." Similar restructuring priorities taking place in the U.K., Australia, New Zealand, and the U.S. had affected South African priorities, with an enhanced role of market-oriented policies. In this light, South Africa's role is less to provide education for empowerment, and more to produce "multi-skilled, flexible and problem-solving workers capable of spearheading South Africa's entry into new markets." Pam Christie of the University of Witwatersrand's Department of Education fundamentally agrees with this viewpoint, noting that academic education and vocational training of a very generic nature have been integrated or converged in many industrial countries, to meet the needs of a "more qualified labor force," at work in more "skill intensive production."

Some analysts have attempted an "Afrocentric" approach toward contemporary South Africa's educational dilemma (Nieuwenhus, 1996), though with limited success and collaborative spirit. Others have largely looked toward the importation of foreign models (Musker, 1997), with similar limitations. What seemed clearest as South Africa was moving from a closed apartheid state to an open, democratic one was that the ANC had few programmatic plans for educational transformation, other than the local reforms already under way in the late 1980s and early 1990s. As University of Western Cape professor Peter Kallaway put it, there was a "tendency to neglect the tradition of educational politics derived from the resistance era," specifically the popular educational campaigns of the UDF and its affiliates. Starkly different from those inspiring projects, "the point of reference for both the ANC and [pro-apartheid] National Party initiatives during the period of transition was often the expertise of international agencies such as the World Bank, the Institute of International Educational Planning, the International Monetary Fund."

The possibilities and promises for postapartheid South Africa are great, as great as were the evils enacted upon the people during the apartheid era. Reaching for those possibilities and meeting even some of those promises present a challenge confused by competing ideologies and a lack of clarity or agreement on what type of transformation should take place. There is little doubt, however, whatever the future holds, that education will be near the center of the most intense struggles for change.

Chapter 4

POSITIVE AND NEGATIVE GLOBALISMS

On the crowded streets of New York City, or in our overcrowded high schools, it is hard to avoid the global community surrounding us. The United Nations, with all its colorful flags, cannot compare with the multitudes of color and contrast on a single subway platform. One can't be a born and raised New Yorker, infused with that open-24-hours energy, or an adopted lover of the city's intensity without having at least some respect for the internationalism that makes our town unique. Yet sociopolitical and economic forces at the dawn of the twenty-first century have captured a buzzword, carrying now consistently negative connotations: globalization. The "globalization" of the world's megabusinesses and its effect on education and other development-based fields have been the cause of rambunctious demonstrations, fervent debates, and now — just beginning — a bit of critical research.

Those Africanists at the forefront of investigation and action regarding the effects of "globalization" on teaching and learning are, in part, collected in *A Thousand Flowers: Social Struggles Against Structural Adjustment in African Universities*, edited by Silvia Federici, George Caffentzis, and Oussania Alidou. As founders and leaders of the Committee for Academic Freedom in Africa (CAFA), they have laid the basis for an overall analysis of the ways in which World Bank (WB) and International Monetary Fund (IMF) programs have hindered the ability of educators everywhere to create meaningful classroom-based social change. That the WB/IMF loans, designed to "adjust" the structures of Third World economic systems, are sometimes touted as educationally sound and supportive suggests the level of disinformation and difference present in Western discussions. Federici, Caffentzis, Alidou, and others not only refute these claims but suggest that the future of African academic freedom and education itself are endangered by structural adjustment and the WB/IMF globalization schemes.

Caffentzis cites numerous WB/IMF reports to conclude that their "picture of campus life is out of touch with reality."[1] Though WB/IMF programs call for austerity in the face of a pessimistic premise of the long-term nature of Africa's economic problems, their proposed solutions are full of contradictions. Indeed, student life on most African campuses is catastrophic — with overcrowding, lack of supplies, failing electricity and water supplies, and collapsing buildings just some of the more pressing issues. Creating new structures, however, that provide for a diminishing amount of funds toward education (in hopes of ultimately creating a small sector of a highly trained African elite) is a "guarantee" — in Caffentzis's view — that African education, "already on the verge of extinction," will ultimately lead to even greater disasters. Noting that, amidst a continent-wide population of 500 million, fewer than 500,000 people were taking part in higher education (a fluctuating rate of between 1 and 2 percent), Caffentzis asserts that "any policy that lowers enrollment rates — hovering now near zero — can be seen as a policy of academic exterminism."[2]

One reason for these policies, accepted by African countries under the threat of starvation or global economic strangulation, is the WB/IMF view of the African nation-state as inherently weak. While there may be some truth to this viewpoint, clearly an anarchist view of decentralized control or an Africanist view of Pan-African unity is not sought out as a solution. Even strengthening the nation-states as clients of the West, a potentially short-term gain for Western capital, is dismissed as unattractive compared to a simpler and more direct economic "integration" and determinism. Thus, African higher education — seen as in the service of bolstering the indigenous bureaucracies and mechanisms of the nation-state — is to be neglected. It is no coincidence here that university students and teachers have been among the harshest critics of WB/IMF structural adjustment — even when the programs don't directly apply to education.

Federici is not the first to term this new process "recolonization." CAFA joined with Africa Watch and other groups throughout the 1980s and 1990s (long before the 1999 anti-IMF "Battle of Seattle") in calling for action on the part of U.S. educators and academics. Africa Watch division director Rakiya Omaar "chastised" the North American academic community for not having given support to the struggles of African students and teachers. He charged them with remaining largely unconcerned or ignorant of the "violation of their colleagues' rights."[3] Recolonization of the political or economic variety, Federici adds, is not the only violation to beware of. An "intellectual recolonization" is also taking place, with an ultimate desire on the part of the WB/IMF to have African education taken over by international agencies.[4] This imagined level of "standardization" and cultural conformity could make even the most callused U.S. educator bristle, but Federici's arguments are backed up by statistics as well as examples. Tanzania's University of Dar es Salaam, a center for critical thinking and Pan-Africanist vision in the 1960s and early 1970s, is now facing material conditions, for example, that make it impossible for "African intellectual workers" to survive. Weekly wages at the university provide for barely three days of subsistence living; all academics (who hardly have access to pens, paper, or books) must work other jobs to maintain their educational commitments and put basic foods on the family table.

However, Federici is quick to point out that these conditions have not been met without resistance. "A new Pan-African student movement," she notes, "continuous in its political aspirations with the student activism that developed in the context of the anticolonial struggle, and yet more radical in its challenge to the established political center,"[5] is beginning to emerge. Though not coordinated by any single organization or international grassroots agency, this movement is united in its motives and objectives and has maintained and increased its networking potential. A 1996 CAFA newsletter listed common slogans that have appeared "on every campus from Lusaka to Cairo in the

1980s and 1990s,"[6] bringing together students and educators too often seen as divided along ethnic, religious, or political grounds. The demands include "No to tuition fees," "No to cuts in books, stationery or transport allowances," "No to structural adjustment programs and the recolonization of Africa," and — most poignantly — "No to starving while studying."

One of the strongest critics of the new globalization has been Patrick Bond, writing from South Africa of the shifts from the ANC's proposed Reconstruction and Development Program of the early 1990s. His assessment of the charge that the ANC had "abandoned" this progressive program "was indeed true in most crucial areas of social policy,"[7] and it is backed up by a look at the field of education. Over several years following the 1994 democratic election, there was a decreased commitment to adult basic education; the special educational needs of disabled students were not "aggressively addressed" as had been promised; the receptor year of compulsory education was not made mandatory; there was a reduced commitment to funding of senior secondary education; and children's rights were not, in Bond's evaluation, coherently addressed. The reasons for this shift, as has already been implied, relate directly to South Africa's growing reliance on and collaboration with the international lending agencies of the West. "South Africa's immediate postapartheid domestic policy," writes Bond, "was excessively influenced by conventional neoliberal wisdom, in many cases imported through 'international experience' (a euphemism for advice by the World Bank and its allies)."[8]

South African analyst Franco Banchiesi uses Bond's characterization of "homegrown structural adjustment" to describe a special case where debt to foreign international agencies is kept low, but a massive public debt is accrued — going to large corporate investors of an all-too-often multinational variety.[9] These debts, it is noted, place a "massive constraint" on South African public expenditure, and Banchiesi cites prominent examples of public funding cutbacks to make his general case. Four years after the end of apartheid, a Presidential Commission of Inquiry had to be called to investigate disturbances and protests at the University of Durban-Westville (UDW). Twelve students and staff were expelled because of their ardent leadership of demonstrations against educational cuts and a narrowing of academic focus. At a college historically segregated for the Indian community under apartheid — but long a site of multiracial struggle — the beginning of repression against democratic expression seemed evident. "The largely yet to be written story of the right-wing shift to neoliberalism in South African tertiary education," writes Banchiesi, "demonstrates that it is possible to analyze neoliberalism and resistance in this country as part of a broad, continent-wide process."[10]

Prominent Egyptian intellectual and activist Samir Amin has used the term "de-linking" to describe the means by which developing nations can and must build institutional alternatives to the present order. "De-linking is the opposite strategy to that proposed by the dominent capitalist forces," Amin has written, "which invite us to 'adjust' to the powerful current flowing from the logic of capitalist expansion." The World Social Forums, initiated by Amin's Senegal-based Third World Forum, have been a major contemporary vehicle for networking among progressive protesters. "De-linking implies requiring the north to adjust to the development of the South," Amin continues. "It's all about working for another globalization."[11]

Two years prior to the UDW protests, this author and colleague Bill Sutherland presented papers at the International Peace Research Association conference, held at Durban-Westville, on the topic of "positive globalization." The university was and remains a sprawling set of small but impressive buildings; it is host to a nongovernmental agency committed to conflict resolution and mediation in the region and to a mini-library dedicated to the legacy of Mohandas Gandhi and former ANC leader Chief Albert Luthuli. Memories of the opening of that library and the high spirits shared by conference attendees from all across the world — joined by the granddaughter of Gandhi (now a South African member of Parliament) and a daughter of Luthuli — flooded back as I learned of the pro-education campaigns and their subsequent state-headed repression. Those lofty men of peace, we remembered at the opening, were well aware that nonviolence could not be achieved in the absence of absolute justice. The economic policies of the WB/IMF, with all their social, cultural, and educational repercussions, are as much a form of violence as the original European scramble to divide up Africa.

Sutherland and I tried to reclaim the term "globalization" and frame a new rhetoric that would reveal the possibilities of united action and Pan-Africanism. Citing three examples from three decades of political tumult, our argument was that positive globalization had a history as well as a future. The Sahara Protests of the 1960s brought African American and European peacemakers together with West African (especially Ghanaian) independentists to march on what was then the French colony of Upper Volta, putting their bodies in the way of French nuclear testing. In this instance, the tests were stopped and the World Peace Brigades movement was born. The anti-apartheid movement, we argued and must not forget, was global in nature — requiring the vigilance and steadfastness of the boycott and divestment campaigns along with and in conjunction with the militant South African exile, underground, and above-ground movements and supported by the frontline states. Finally, the largely Internet-based campaign against the Multilateral Agreement on Investment (MAI), an offshoot of WB/IMF policies, showed that even in the early 1990s, progressive campaigns could cross boundaries and have noticeable effects; though replaced by other programs, MAI was substantially stalled by the computer-connected protestors.

One doesn't have to be a Nobel Prize-winning economist to understand that educational priorities are seriously askew when they are based on short-term profit, rather than on the social betterment of the planet, on new and creative forms of self-expression, or on major breakthroughs in science or medicine. It doesn't hurt, however, when even the recent U.S. Nobel laureates come forth with their critiques — as did former World Bank head Joseph Stiglitz in a scathing indictment of his previous employer and the spreading of "globalization and its discontents," or California-based Joseph Akerlof, who was famously quoted late in 2003 as calling the George W. Bush administration the "worst presidency" in the history of the U.S.[12] Documenting the impact of the global economy on local communities within the U.S., National Association for Bilingual Education vice president Carlo Mitton correctly diagnosed the trend as having "far-reaching implications," especially in communities of color, where calls for the privatization of failing schools and collusion between corporate raiders and school administration officials have become the norm.[13] Mitton examined the well-paid but largely unestablished work of Edison Schools, Inc., the largest for-profit manager of schools in the U.S. With losses in community control (or input) in schools; shifting (and diminished) emphasis on research-based, developmentally appropriate language instruction; and general institutional neglect of inner-city public schools, Mitton correctly concluded that the New World Order's politics of greed had placed "the fate of the American system of public education in the balance."[14]

Positive globalization will be necessary in any campaign for forward-looking education, especially in light of the policies of the negative, globalized economic monoliths that are more commonly thought of. Complete, intercontinentally integrated internationalism, across all the vast divides that have historically kept movements apart, may not be the first step. A positive globalized Pan-Africanism, however, may be closer to a realizable goal — as students, teachers, and concerned community members realize that there is little left to lose.

SECTION II

EDUCATIONAL ALTERNATIVES

Chapter 5

PAN-AFRICANISM AND AFRICANIST PHILOSOPHIES OF EDUCATION

Misunderstood and confused in the U.S.-based debates surrounding "Afrocentrism," the ideals of a Pan-Africanist perspective — seriously developed in the era of decolonization of Africa that took place in the second half of the twentieth century — cry out for further investigation when searching for educational alternatives. While Asante, Jeffries, and others challenged academics to place Africa firmly at the "center" of world history and development,[1] and their detractors from both liberal and conservative camps suggested that such a placement would at least rob a generation of students of true cultural literacy and at worst serve as a divisive wedge between the peoples of "these United States,"[2] the real contributions of African academic and educational leaders were left unpublicized, often unnoticed. Though some of these Pan-Africanist writers did push for a historical review of ancient Africa that would challenge a Eurocentric model on anthropological and political grounds,[3] the majority of African teachers and scholars were looking not for center stage but for a unified educational development model that would move forward the teaching of African peoples throughout the world. Before reviewing country-specific attempts at African educational reforms, and their relevancy to our work in the U.S., it is imperative to recognize the Pan-Africanist viewpoint.

Modern Pan-Africanist thought has been most influenced by the scholarship and actions of the U.S.'s W. E. B. Du Bois and Ghana's Kwame Nkrumah. Du Bois's extraordinary academic curriculum vitae — at Harvard, in his groundbreaking writings on Black Reconstruction, and in his commentaries of the political and economic trends of the day (including but not exclusive to a view of the significance of Africa)[4] — have earned him a place as one of the great twentieth-century thinkers of any race or region. Nkrumah, more the man of action (originally labeled the Gandhi of Africa because of his nonviolent "positive action" plan for the independence of the Gold Coast),[5] is as well known today for his championing of the concept of a United States of Africa as he is for the importance of being the first to lead his country into the postcolonial era. Many suggest that the eventual coup that deposed Nkrumah from his native Ghana for the last years of his life was at least in part possible because of his intense focus on the affairs of the continent rather than the narrow interests of the political elites at home.[6] In any case, two points are clear and extraordinary about Nkrumah's last years. First, the colonial powers that were on the move and the imperialist powers that were taking their place in the post-World War II scene felt threatened by Nkrumah's increasing radicalism and influence on independence movements throughout the Global South, in particular Africa. His scholarly *Neocolonialism* predicted trends that IMF/World Bank and world trade critics of the current period can still use to understand the process of "late capitalism." His revolutionary "little black book" — predating Mao Tse Tung's book of a different color — was being passed around Africa as well as Asia and the Pacific.[7] Secondly, Nkrumah's Pan-Africanist vision was not limited to theory alone; the historically unprecedented solidarity act of neighboring Guinean president Sekou Toure — making Nkrumah (in exile from Ghana) the co-president of Guinea — has yet to be equaled in any part of the planet. For those years, in that region of West Africa, the Pan-Africanist model was put into practical effect.

Du Bois challenged educators and academics by suggesting that the fundamental problem of the twentieth century was the problem of the color line. Though committed to his U.S. roots, and to the organization (the National Association for the Advancement of Colored People) that he spent decades building and leading, Du Bois decided to spend his last days in Africa, making an important symbolic link for African Americans of the day. He died on the eve of the historic 1963 March on Washington (where Dr. Martin Luther King, Jr., delivered his "I Have a

Dream" speech), never witnessing the dramatic changes of the late civil rights and early Black liberation movement periods. Nkrumah's challenge to teachers and statesmen focused more on the need for a principled and organizationally based unity among all people of African descent. This all-African dream, while resulting in the development of several international groups, some of which are still in operation, has been largely unrealized.

Significantly, both of these most crucial Pan-Africanist challenges had little to do with a narrow Africanist provincialism or sectarianism. Though concerned first and foremost with the needs of their own people, both Du Bois and Nkrumah intentionally distanced themselves from what might be considered separatist or Afrocentric racialist approaches. The movements of Marcus Garvey in the West and Leopold Senghor on the continent, though part of the larger Pan-Africanist canon, were fundamentally different than the internationalism of Du Bois, Nkrumah, and their colleagues.[8] Garvey's Back to Africa and Senghor's Negritude, forerunners of the Afrocentric educational movements of the 1980s, enjoyed mass appeal generated largely through the charismatic leadership of these two figures. Du Bois and Nkrumah, on another level entirely, held world conferences that brought together unparalleled groupings of African leaders from every corner of the earth. It was never so much that peoples of European descent should not be allowed on the basis of race or ethnicity — but rather that race-consciousness and unity among Africans would be required to counterbalance the power of the Eurocentric political economies. For white folks with an understanding of the primacy of the problem of race and a respect for the needs of Africanists to unite, international solidarity, communication, and camaraderie were always a possibility for the Pan-Africanism of Du Bois and Nkrumah.

Understanding Pan-Africanism within this framework is essential for all educators attempting to avoid a so-called "Balkanized" world view and to avoid actual Balkanization among students and teachers in our diverse and often divided institutions. Multicultural and alternative education, for example, was never intended to create a pretense for the ahistorical methodologies of "every culture treated equally," as in the food festivals and fairs where everyone has a dish on a table, but no true comparative study is done. Similarly, multiculturalism was never intended by most to be a simple bringing together of critical fields, such as African American studies, Latino/Hispanic studies, women's studies, etc. The progressive pedagogical approach of James Banks's transformative and social change models,[9] along with the research of Grant, Sleeter, and others[10] that backs up this approach, is a multiculturalism that looks at the roots of power within society and our school systems — and calls for a justice-seeking "new balance" of power. This approach bears much similarity to the progressive Pan-Africanism of Du Bois, Nkrumah, and their followers in that it moves toward fundamental and radical change, embracing a long-term vision of peace and prosperity among diverse peoples. This is not to say that there is only one single "correct" way to bring about the empowerment of a people or a single "successful" level or method of multicultural and alternative education. It is simply to suggest that this "progressive Pan-Africanism," like Banks's transformative multicultural education, holds greater possibility for lasting educational reform and social liberation than ideologies with less holistic and historical points of view.

Modern proponents of Pan-Africanism understand, to a large extent, the difficulties of standing up against a globalized culture and political economy from the point of view of a single nation-state or region. Educators from the West — including most alarmingly but not exclusively, social studies practitioners — have long had a problem with understanding African contributions in an appropriate context. Aside from the basic lessons of the Kush in teaching science or the Benin math initiatives of ancient times, simple modern geography is mangled by some of our best minds, who can't seem to help equating a land mass three and one-half times the size of the continental U.S. with a single city. Afrocentrism, to be sure, rarely helps with these basic problems, as Africa itself has several centers. Basic cultural literacy, to steal a phrase, should be more bound up in a careful understanding of the several centers of African power: South Africa, to be sure, but also Ghana, Nigeria, and Senegal in the west; Egypt, Libya, and the Islamic influence in the north; Congo as a central state;

Tanzania and the regionalization attempts in the east; Ethiopia, Eritrea, and the budding language study initiatives in the Horn. These six African centers of power, within the Pan-Africanist framework, are key for both Western educators and academics seeking to share resources and success stories based on mutual understanding. This sharing, in turn, becomes key in creating a world that celebrates equity through multicultural awareness rather than attempting homogeneity through globalization.

Unsurprisingly, contemporary Pan-African advocates place special emphasis on the importance of education and consciousness. Trinidadian-born Stokely Carmichael, whose leadership of the student wing of mainstream civil rights politics created the platform for his internationally recognized influence, came to represent the all-African aspirations of the older generation. Carmichael, onetime national leader of the Student Nonviolent Coordinating Committee and early proponent of Black Power, took on the name Kwame Ture in deference to his Ghanaian and Guinean mentors. Throughout his travels and writings of the 1980s and '90s, Ture maintained a consistent focus on the significance of student and youth leadership and had his greatest base among college and high school Black teacher and student clubs. Even as an advanced cancer weakened him in his last days in New York, he made a priority to have a final discussion with America's young people — and set up a meeting with a dozen students from various alternative schools.[11] His emphasis that students and teachers must not simply talk about change, but also organize and join organizations — whether they be a local neighborhood, community, or church group or a union or after-school club or political party — echoed his longstanding Pan-Africanist goals. "Organization precedes unity," he suggested, because unless a people join together they cannot easily unite with others.[12] The organization of people within formal and informal educational institutions remained a driving theme of Ture's till the end.

A number of leading contemporary educational theorists from Africa echo the Pan-Africanist priorities of consciousness, organization, and unity. In their teacher-trainer-oriented *Towards an African Philosophy of Education*, N. Q. Mkabela and P. C. Luthuli begin with the icon of African teacher-statesmen, Julius Nyerere, who stated that "the purpose of education is to transmit from one generation to the next, the accumulated wisdom and knowledge of society, and to prepare the young people for their future membership of the society and their active participation in its maintenance or development."[13] A secondary school educator, Nyerere went on to lead the independence struggle in his country of birth and became first president of free Tanganyika, later united with Zanzibar to become Tanzania. The Tanzanian experiments with regional indigenous forms of education and literary and social organization were some of the most ambitious to be attempted in the postindependence period; today it remains one of the few countries to have two official languages: English along with the native Swahili.

Speaking of transition of accumulated wisdom and active social participation, Nyerere summarized an educational philosophy that is essentially values-driven and civically oriented. A society, any society, that cuts off the possibilities of a new generation's political, economic, or cultural participation has also moved away from democracy and education for empowerment. African or otherwise, such education may only serve baser needs: to create an obedient and reliable labor force, to select a "best and brightest" core of specialists, to separate an elite from an underclass. In Africa, Nyerere's educational approach — as in other areas — was to mix the traditional and indigenous with modern and Western models. The Africanist nature of his educational approach was essentially to create an open, democratic, and proud population — even in the context of possible poverty and underdevelopment. In a private conversation with this author, Nyerere discussed the basic simplicity of this plan and the many difficulties of implementation. The declarations and alternative methodologies, he reflected, were easy to draw up and ultimately deemed failures at the first setback. In truth, however, most of his initiatives were never tried.[14] Nevertheless, Tanzania to this day is one of the few developing countries that has made smooth and regular electoral transitions from one ruling group to another. And it is fitting that Julius Nyerere's sentimental legacy is not to be called "Mahatma" (great soul), or some grandiose title, but "Mwalimu" — the Swahili word for teacher. Nonetheless, even in Tanzania, there have been some recent shifts away from "Siasa" — political education — taught in Kiswahili, toward English-language civics education preparing youngsters for the "global village."

Mkabela and Luthuli extend Nyerere's original philosophy by emphasizing the need for an education that serves the common good of any country or region. As far as race and culture are concerned, they note that it is common for a broadly defined, multicultural education to be proposed for modern African nation-states, and they attempt to define an African philosophy of education in part by investigating what multicultural is and what it is not. For multiculturalism to be more than temporary, conflict avoidance-oriented myth, those setting up educational institutions must look at what common root values exist among a given diverse population within an African country or area.[15] If administrators attempt to look at both common as well as distinct values, to utilize African methodologies as well as address more universal questions, then a unique African philosophy of education may emerge. Too often, they assert, what is called multicultural education loses its focus in diluted, feel-good, same-size-fits-all policies.[16]

These valid critiques are somewhat muddied in Mkabele and Luthuli's attempts to quantify this so-called African "philosophy of education," which is little more than progressive educational principles applied to a Pan-Africanist perspective. In their conclusion, Mkabela and Luthuli suggest that African education, in its concern with the prevailing circumstances in Africa, must "try and recapture any democratic elements in African culture."[17] The true philosophy here is that of Nyerere, Du Bois, and Nkrumah — applied to an educational framework. In that, their work provides a valuable first step.

John K. Marah takes these efforts to the next level. He begins, explicitly as a Pan-Africanist, reviewing the division of the continent from the time of the scramble for Africa to the present "reinforcement" that he perceives current leaders to be engaged in. He goes on to analyze the fact that "current educational schemes in Africa emphasize academic education for those who have already proven themselves capable of succeeding anywhere." Vocational education is almost impossible to find and is largely inaccessible to the majority of the continent's population living in rural areas. While acknowledging that tribal educational systems functioned well in particular stages of historic development, Marah does not romanticize: "Tribal systems of education have proven themselves inadequate for modern technological societies."[18]

Recent research on the continent has underscored the contemporary needs facing developing societies. Catherine Odora-Hoppers, Ugandan-born United Nations Commissioner on Education for All, has written poignantly that the African voice in education is the voice of "the radical witness of the pain and inhumanity of history, the arrogance of modernization and the conspiracy of silence in academic disciplines toward what is organic and alive in Africa."[19] Attempts to "retrieve the past, engage the present, and shape the future" have centered on the need to sychronize education and development policy, to develop massive public campaigns for education, to design curricula to fit specific development needs, and to create balances between the humanities, math and science, and inclusive language policies.[20] Symposia and conferences have brought together educators from various disciplines to build programs beyond country- or region-specific models. More often than not, these "radical witnesses" have come up with consistent critiques of what has been termed "two irreconcilable trends." The alternative to globalization, on the one hand, is a continental education policy genuinely concerned with "good governance, democracy, poverty alleviation, and social justice." In the writings of prominent peace and education researcher Birgit Brock-Utne and many Pan-Africanist scholars, this alternative must fundamentally result in "the strengthening of African languages."[21] Moreover, cutting edge scholarship has placed greater emphasis on the importance of indigenous knowledge systems. A "chorus of disaffection" among African scholars and educators has led to significant dialogue and writing on forging forward-looking policies for the benefit of the majority of the people.[22]

John Marah's important *Pan-African Education: The Last Stage of Educational Developments in Africa* (1989), though dated, still serves as a significant, guiding framework. He concludes that Pan-African education needs to be secular in nature and practical in its approaches toward unity, and it must serve as a foundation for other institutions throughout African societies. Looking at African integration as a necessary step for empowerment and development, Marah suggests that "the schools are the starting place" for effective and dedicated teachers, administrators, and other school personnel to create a united Africa, "in diversity with vivacity."[23] He advocates, as did Nkrumah and Ethiopia's Selassie,[24] an all-African integrated university and boldly states that "until African illiteracy is drastically reduced, abominable leaders...will continue to misrule and mismanage Africa's natural resources and justify Western European negative attitudes towards Africa and African people whenever they are."[25] While never disregarding neocolonialism's overall responsibility for Africa's current plight, Marah sees Pan-Africanist education as a twenty-first–century solution for dealing with the challenges of an increasingly dichotomized and unequal world.

Supporting this position, Maya Angelou has suggested that a thorough program of Pan-Africanist education has never been adequately attempted. A celebrated author, famous for documenting her own travails and travels to Africa and throughout the U.S., Angelou is an innovative and passionate educator. In discussions with this author and Bill Sutherland, another African American with extensive experience in Africa, Angelou noted that there was no thorough and comprehensive teaching program that explained the lessons of the U.S. civil rights and African postindependence era in a meaningful context for today's youth.[26] In short, the possibilities for this generation to appreciate past contributions and thereby understand civics and the imperatives for current social contributions are limited. Sutherland, who moved to Ghana in 1953 and has lived in Tanzania (as a colleague of Nyerere and a member of the civil service) since the early 1960s, takes a more cynical view. "There have been interesting alternatives attempted in various African countries," he stated, "which have been largely thwarted by the West. And the Black youth of America seem largely uninterested in activism and internationalism."[27]

Sutherland's long history in education and the African–African American connection make his views hard to refute; he served as host to Martin Luther King, Jr., Malcolm X, and many others on their first trips to the continent, and his daughter Esi — now a professor at the University of Legon — has recently served as Ghana's deputy minister of education. In fact Esi's mother, Efua Sutherland, a close associate of Nkrumah, is considered to this day as a "founding mother" of modern Ghanaian education. As a playwright and children's book author, Efua used innovative theatrical techniques to spread formal education throughout the newly independent Ghana of the 1950s and '60s. However, Angelou's positions bear much thought and investigation. The innovations of Ghana, or even of the more recently independent governments of Zimbabwe or Namibia,[28] while substantial and often inspiring, create at best a new curriculum with progressive, pro-African content. A more holistic and inclusive systemwide campaign of regional and global curriculum content changes (utilizing a view of the world with many "centers," not just one or two), as well as teacher-training and administrative overhaul, as Angelou and the Pan-Africanists have proposed, has never really been attempted. In this light, those U.S. students who have sought out a sense of their own history have done so largely based on their own initiatives, without the tools an earlier generation of educational and social reformers might have supplied. It is still worthwhile to examine successful local or country-specific models, with an eye toward replicating best practices and improving education everywhere. Significant changes, however, will be nearly impossible to carry out without a more internationalist, including Pan-Africanist, viewpoint.

Chapter 6

AN ADDITIONAL "R": RECONCILIATION, EDUCATION, AND EMPOWERMENT IN POST-APARTHEID SOUTH AFRICA

When the new South African government took power, following the dramatic democratic elections of 1994 after decades of apartheid rule, education was a major governmental priority. Though cries came out for radical changes from every sector of society and broad policies had to be made specific, the Department of Education — with close to half a million employees — was clearly the largest government division.[1] The first minister of education, S. M. E. Bengu, admitted that the transition to nonracialist education was a process of "magnitude and complexity" confronting no other government service; he nevertheless held his hopes and ambitions high, stating: "Our country is in dire need of men and women who have skills that will assist the country to develop into a giant."[2]

In order to transform one of history's most divided national education systems into not only a coherent and equitable whole but a leader among world systems, the federal government, in addition to dismantling the assorted Afrikaans-speaking, English, Colored, Indian, and African (Xhosa, Zulu, etc.) systems, had to construct an organized plan. The Department of Education (DOE) — including a minister, a deputy minister, and a director-general — presided over four major branches of postapartheid education. The Education and Training Systems branch became the heart of the new plan, with a Constitutional Courts decree, initiatives on the cultures of learning and international liaisons, a school building and nutrition program, and a special needs focus. The General and Further Education branch served as brain, of sorts, for the plan — with a view that all South Africans be treated as "lifelong learners situated within empowering frameworks"[3] and with a Curriculum 2005 project, early childhood and adult educational programs, and a focus on language in education. The Higher Education branch looked at systemic and institutional ways in which the DOE could assist South Africa's universities and colleges on a path of self-transformation, including a focus on teacher education. Finally, the Human Resources and Administration branch was to handle basic management development issues, with a special focus on gender equity in education.

The first significant challenge of the new DOE came from legislative quarters. Minority parties in the new parliament challenged the constitutionality of a proposed South African Schools Act that, in essence, simply called for a uniform system of nondiscriminatory education, with organization and funding centrally controlled. While parliamentary detractors — holdovers from the apartheid right-wing and some narrow nationalist advocates — suggested that the act impinged on the "legislative competence" of provincial and local governments and gave too much authority to the minister of education and DOE, the act's supporters stated grandiosely that the bill would place South Africa "in the forefront of education reform."[4] Ultimately, the Constitutional Court upheld the act, noting that it required the DOE to undertake a consultative process in determining educational policy. With the establishment of both a Council of Education Ministers drawn from throughout the country and a Head of Departments of Education Committee, President Mandela signed the National Education Policy Act into law in 1996. It paved the way for the DOE to continue its "branch focus" plans but was no sweeping or radical policy initiative in itself. It was, to be sure, explicitly anti-apartheid and pro-equality.

One positive outgrowth of the Constitutional Court controversy and debate was a series of public meetings held in late 1996 in over fifty regional centers. With copies of the act sent to 29,000 public schools and countless principals, educators, governing bodies, learners, and other "educational stakeholders," over sixty meetings took place, with a wide range of concerns and needs raised and discussed. These were followed by fifteen nationally convened DOE meetings of regional representatives, who reviewed more than 1,200 written submissions on policy. The 1996 DOE report and subsequent DOE planning were to take these suggestions and this process into account.[5]

By far the most ambitious specific national initiative of the 1994-96 period was the National Schools Building Program, where well over one billion rand was allocated to construct or repair schools in rural areas, townships, and the most underdeveloped parts of the country. Though less than one-third of these monies was actually spent by 1997, the need for a special emphasis on the poorest communities had been set as a priority.

Curriculum 2005, on the other hand, while touted during this period as the fundamental means for implementing DOE's commitment to transformation, was little more than a vague emphasis on outcomes-based education and a merging of academic education and vocational training. Eight learning areas were targeted: language, literacy, and communication; mathematical literacy, mathematics, and mathematical sciences; human and social sciences; natural sciences; technology; arts and culture; economic and management sciences; and life orientation. Beginning with grades one and seven in 1998, these areas were to be incorporated into all schools and all grades, with new curriculum in place, by 2005. It was not overtly clear how this curriculum would be written or implemented, nor were initiatives in lifelong learning or language-in-education spelled out.

This early period can be characterized as a pull-and-tug between the old defenders of apartheid, who wished their basic policies to continue through however subtler or more covert means, and the new government leadership. These leaders — some reformers who had been in exile for much of their lives, others guerrilla fighters, a few who were actually education policy analysts — had much invested in staking and stating their claims: that the days when education for the majority of the population meant disempowerment and disrespect were over. In light of this battle, some unclear or unimplementable specific policies must be critiqued but also forgiven. There was a larger concern to be addressed. "The task of transformation must not be derailed or distracted by disruptive or unlawful activities," demanded Minister Bengu, "by those who prefer coercion to reasoned argument, or by the active or passive resistance of those who have not adjusted to a democratic South Africa based on the equal rights of all persons."[6]

One of the most successful and long-lasting of these original plans was the campaign for a Culture of Learning, Teaching, and Service, documented in a DOE national strategy booklet published with support of the U.S. Agency for International Development.[7] Stating that the interconnectedness of education and service was, indeed, the *raison d'être* of the DOE, the culture of learning served to act, in the department's own words, as "a vanguard activity that mobilizes political, popular and professional energies," thus accelerating the achievement of DOE goals.[8] Father Smengoliso Mkhatshwa, the populist anti-apartheid activist and deputy minister of education from 1994 to the present (the only top DOE official to serve both Mandela and Mbeki), can appropriately be credited with taking a largely rhetorical set of materials and ideas and creating local programs that encouraged the spread of education by means appropriate to those communities most in need.

Mkhatshwa's work notwithstanding, the critiques from within progressive circles only grew as President Mandela's term of office came to a close. A report of Mandela's Presidential Education Initiative Research Project, jointly published by the DOE and an independent body — the Joint Education Trust (JET) — *Getting Learning Right*, served as the catalyst for much of the most public and vociferous controversies.[9] Edited and largely authored by JET's Nick Taylor and Penny Vinjevold, the report took apart DOE's unsuccessful initiatives, at once giving voice to many grassroots criticisms that had been developing since 1994 and also embarrassing the new educational leadership in front of the international community (that Mandela was so lauded for wooing and satisfying).

Getting Learning Right took particular aim at Curriculum 2005. Beginning with a useful overview of curriculum models, Taylor describes two particularly distinct approaches: competence and performance models. Competence models, developed most extensively in the United Kingdom in the 1960s and early '70s, are student-centered and "based on an empancipatory vision in which learners take control of their own learning"[10] in active, creative, and self-regulatory ways. Teachers are essentially facilitators, and education is directed toward what students know and can do at the end of learning. Performance models focus on content and texts and a specific body of knowledge that learners ultimately need to know by the end of the formal schooling process. Most interestingly, Taylor distinguishes three often interconnected subcategories of the South African-oriented competence approach: a liberal/progressive form that emphasizes cognitive empowerment, a populist form that focuses on cultural empowerment, and a radical mode that is the basis for political empowerment. Curriculum 2005, in its own terminology, attempted "the most radical form of an integrated curriculum," seeking to integrate all eight learning areas in all educational activities, grades one through twelve. This, according to the DOE, would produce a "profound transferability of knowledge in real life."[11]

Taylor begins by recognizing that the implementation program of Curriculum 2005 is "enormously complex,"[12] with sixty-six specific outcomes across the eight learning areas for grades one through three. Citing Ted Sizer's "less is more" approach that students should master, in depth, a limited number of essential skills — with curricular decisions guided according to student mastery of these skills — Taylor notes that U.S. education has been criticized for covering a large range of topics superficially. According to the Third International Mathematics and Science Study (TIMSS), also cited by Taylor, the general U.S. curriculum model (if such a thing can be said to exist) is "a mile wide and an inch deep."[13] Using a similar analytic tool, Taylor and colleagues suggest that South Africa's Curriculum 2005 covers "at least as diverse a range of topics"[14] as the U.S. curriculum studied by TIMSS. "Curriculum 2005," Taylor concludes, "seems designed to promote superficiality at the expense of systematic and grounded conceptual development."[15] In this way, proponents of neither competence-based nor performance models — the left and the right of curriculum development — would be satisfied. Teachers, students, parents, and community members, it should be added, would face a similar dissatisfaction.

Generally speaking, the perspective of *Getting Learning Right* accepts that "there is a broad consensus that teaching and learning in the majority of South African schools leaves much to be desired. The problems are generally described in terms of teacher-centeredness, pupil passivity, rote learning, and the like."[16] Their findings indicated that lessons were dominated by teacher-talk and low-level questions; that little reading, writing, or group work is done by pupils; and that while real-world examples are often used in the classroom, they are presented at a very superficial level. Wrong answers were "not infrequently" marked correct, new assessment modes were unclear and unworkable, and a generally undereducated teaching staff, "without a secure knowledge base to build on," would not greatly benefit from simple in-service training.[17] In general, though stamped with the prestige of being part of the President's Education Initiative, *Getting Learning Right* presented a bleak view of the federal government's attempt at reform during its first five years, inciting the ire of many top- and middle-level officials.

With the election of President Thabo Mbeki in mid-1999, the still-ruling African National Congress leadership assumed a mandate to continue their basic policies, along with a need to implement them at an "accelerated delivery" rate. At his first cabinet meeting as president, Mbeki asked his new education minister, Professor Kader Asmal, whether South Africans were truly educationally prepared for the twenty-first century. Asmal declined to answer, setting up a monthlong "listening period" before producing his own call to action — which, on July 27, 1999, described the educational condition of the majority of South Africans as being in a state of "national emergency."

Asmal's Call to Action, while accepting that the country had "strong, committed leadership and excellent policies and laws," suggested also that the system was "seriously dysfunctional" with "crisis at all levels."[18] From his perspective, the main problems included rampant inequality, low teacher morale, failures of governance and management, and poor quality of learning. A new mobilization campaign was set up for DOE under the slogan "Tirisano" — working together. Tirisano included an emphasis on administrative assistance to the provincial education departments, ending illiteracy in a five-year period, transforming schools into centers of community cultural life, and — again — taking care of the "physical degradation" that had been the fate of so many school buildings and rooms.

The 1999 DOE Annual Report frankly reviewed the critiques of *Getting Learning Right* and the problems of Curriculum 2005. The report openly stated that many within and outside the DOE had concluded that "curriculum transformation would shipwreck on the rock of teachers' ignorance and on the inadequacy of official attempts to improve and sustain their efforts to cope with radical change."[19] On the one hand, the DOE noted that the President's Education Initiative was limited in its set-up and did not attempt to create a representative sample of schools they were studying. On the other, the DOE suggested that "taken on its own" it was not news that many primary schools were providing inadequate services. DOE committed itself to conducting more broadly representative research and to review the examples of teachers and learners who had succeeded "against the odds."

The 1999 report, and subsequent governmental actions, reaffirmed a focus on learning outcomes, admitting that a move away from the "tyranny of the syllabus" represented radical change, and therefore a careful look at the concepts set forth for possible outcomes was required. Nationally agreed on learning outcomes would be based on provincial departments and schools, and more detailed guidelines on learning objectives, content, and pedagogy were produced. Within teacher education, new "Norms and Standards for Educators" became policy in 2000, with an articulation that these norms would serve as a starting point for strengthening teacher development. There were also efforts to rectify a major source of national anger and embarrassment — the delay in getting textbooks and basic supplies to schools for the first day of classes — with some improvement over the last two years. In general, however, it appears to be too soon to tell how successful the new and renewed DOE initiatives of 1999 have been.

One undeniable root of the problem, addressed in the 1999 report and numerous speeches and articles, was the enormous systemic nature of the educational transitions being attempted with regard to race and diversity. The DOE suggested that the unprecedented demographic upheaval in education since the end of apartheid had the "characteristics of a spontaneous migratory movement rather than a planned process of social integration."[20] While contemporary South African educational leaders on the national level were quick to insist that human rights play a strong part in all curricular and systemic reforms, they nevertheless were cautious in focusing on racism as "the most grievous of social ills." In an ironic and potentially dangerous analysis, many placed racism as only a manifestation of antidemocratic and antisocial values. Unfortunately, in the country whose history has been most marked by racial division and whose very basis has been constructed on theories of racial/ethnic particularities, any broad initiative — like federal education reform — that doesn't deal squarely with this past may be doomed by its limitations. One doesn't have to accept those outdated concepts of African or Indian or Colored or white capacity to learn in order to accept that racism was at the core of decades of educational policy; any policy looking to reverse those decades of indoctrination must surely address how racism continues to be a part of the socioeducational structures at all levels. Despite many exciting changes, and a refreshing ability to engage in self-critique and refinement, the postapartheid national education agencies have yet to consistently and systemically address this question.

* * *

In the classrooms of KwaZulu/Natal, or in the town of Mpumalonga, national South African educational initiatives, be they linked to Curriculum 2005 or not, are centered around a new mode of teaching and assessment. Outcome-Based Education and Training (OBET), developed extensively in Europe, Australia, and the U.S., began being implemented in grades one and eight shortly after the 1994 elections — and 1998 was the year of transformation. As with other initiatives at the federal level, OBET had a significant group of supporters and critics among the national leadership. On the grassroots level, there was at least verbal approval, along with some questions and concerns. In the words of one first grade teacher, "You find it very noisy, and when you're trying to teach, you're to do different things with different groups." It was a "very noisy OBE."[21]

OBET has surely been one of the national programs most widely implemented over the past several years. As such, its standing as a progressive alternative teaching and assessment model is significant in looking at South Africa's overall progress. Cliff Malcolm notes that OBET itself has a number of different forms and interpretations. With few "pure" educational models, OBET is, in his view, "invariably system-centered in the sense of working to prescribed outcomes according to the OBET model in use,"[22] but that does not mean that the school system or administration itself controls everything going on in the school. Insofar as Curriculum 2005 makes a strong distinction between inputs and outcomes, giving schools the responsibility for developing inputs that conform to nationally defined outcomes, C2005 can be said to be outcome-based. But, as Malcolm clarifies, it is also learner-centered, with desired outcomes focusing on the need for students to demonstrate how technology might reflect different biases and create responsible and ethical strategies to prevent them, or to demonstrate an understanding of the historical development of math in diverse cultural contexts, or to respect people's rights to have personal beliefs and values.[23] In his view, this OBET takes an "organic" approach, putting learners first, envisioning a heterogeneous classroom of students moving at different speeds — as individuals and in small-group settings — to master a series of progressively demanding activities in relation to progressively sophisticated learning outcomes. If, however, teachers begin to use national government learning programs and guidelines but do not look for common assessment tools and models, C2005 may be competence based and learner centered, but not truly outcome based.

A strong proponent of OBET is Haroon Mahomed of the Gauteng Institute for Curriculum Development (GICD). Asserting that OBET in South Africa *has* to succeed in order to make a clean break from apartheid education, Mahomed suggests that rather than look pessimistically at why OBET may fail, educators, administrators, and policy makers have to rethink a variety of assumptions about both the meaning of OBET and the nature of possibility in a new South Africa. The areas of "rethinking" recommended by Mahomed include the following: that *all* learners can learn and succeed, though at different rates and in different ways; that success breeds success and that local schools and teachers control the conditions for student success; that learners should collaborate rather than compete; and that no one should be excluded. These basic educational principles, while definitely student-centered, can be part of any OBET program, but they are not fundamental to it. Nonetheless, in Mahomed's view, "The appeal of OBET for South Africa lies in its potential to address our critical educational problems. The emphasis in OBET on accountability, equity, positivity, mix of control and local responsibility and competence, changed roles and responsibilities of teachers, learners, and communities and on the significance of what is being learned, lends itself to responding to many of our educational concerns."[24]

Typifying a somewhat different tendency, University of Durban-Westville's Jonathan D. Jansen has written extensively on why OBET will certainly fail. A coeditor with Wits University's Pam Christie of *Changing Curriculum: Studies on Outcomes-Based Education in South Africa*, Jansen has conducted research in his own Durban/Natal region suggesting that, even within a given school, educators have widely different understandings of what OBET is. "Teachers referred to OBET in terms common to most progressive pedagogy everywhere," he wrote, rather than to the specific mastery skills intended by the DOE.[25] Blaming this on a lack of DOE coherence and focus, Jansen at one point summarizes that while teachers claimed that they were utilizing different practices under OBET, in fact they were teaching much as they had before.[26] On close examination, however, Jansen's own research points to a variety of actual and significant changes. Teachers were teaching less, serving as guides to small student groups, and being more flexible with the structure of the school day. Students were being encouraged, with some success, to use "multiple representational contexts" for their tasks, with less exclusive reliance on written papers and tests. Life skills were being more deliberately included in the local curriculum.

While Jansen suggests that some of the above changes were simply being talked about and not widely implemented, still significant — over a relatively short period of time — are a variety of progressive reforms found to be present in some form at the grassroots level. As Malcolm's less sectarian essay points out, these shifts may have less to do with OBET and more with a commitment to and understanding of student-centered and competence-based education. However, these reforms are not contradictory to OBET and, in some ways, may be an important early step in transforming the curriculum, student expectations, and teacher readiness in the direction of a more traditional and overt OBET approach.

A more even-handed and certainly forward-looking approach is taken by Meg Pahad of South Africa's Independent Examinations Board. Her own chief concern, that outcome-based assessment be a key component of any OBET program, led her to examine the evolution of policy and opinion on assessment, concluding in 1999 that "at last consensus is emerging about several broad principles."[27] Specifically, the need to make assessment criteria explicit, to use assessment developmentally, and to make the process as transparent as possible seemed common ground for all those advocating a South African education system based on quality, relevance, equity, and access. Beyond these basic principles, Pahad puts forth that "the main question the teacher needs to be able to answer in an OBET system is 'how far along the continuum of increasingly complex performance the learner has progressed in relation to the outcomes which have been selected as the focus of the section.'"[28] The fears that OBET would result in easily measurable, demonstrable, and "scientific" standardized testing materials are unfounded; though not yet in place, the nationally agreed-upon outcomes in a variety of areas of learning specifically point to a diversity of measurement modalities and an acceptance of varying levels of standards. Assessment tools have to be prepared, on the school level, with teachers playing the key role in ensuring that student input not be lost in the OBET process. Referencing her own organization's work, Pahad notes that GICD itself has been constructing progress maps to help teachers define outcomes and utilize assessment measurements in systematic and structured ways. Gauteng suggests that a cycle of "assess, plan, implement, reflect" be introduced.[29] Finally, like her Gauteng colleagues, Pahad emphasizes that in contemporary South Africa there is "no viable alternative" to OBET. "We have no choice," she writes, "but to find the resources, the political will, the energy and the commitment to make OBET succeed."[30]

Like so many debates in South African society, the discussions around Outcomes-Based Education and Training seem unnecessarily polarized. Even with the educational elite and teacher-training institutes, terminology is often used loosely and incomplete research applied too universally. While principles are not the same as practice, substantial change anywhere takes time as well as understanding, and a particular method — good or bad — need not be used conclusively to condemn or applaud an entire process. OBET, undoubtedly, is an important part of South Africa's current attempts at educational change, but it is not the entirety of DOE or grassroots alternative initiatives. Two years into the OBET experiment, there are signs of problems and misunderstandings, but there are also clearly success stories and valiant attempts being made. While the long-denied majority of South Africans rightfully demand fast-paced initiatives, for the aforementioned elite to help support change in the most constructive means possible is vital. There is no doubt that changes will take place. One can be certain, at least, that the inevitable educational transformation of South Africa will be a very noisy process indeed. To what extent progressive shifts led by national DOE leaders are able to prevail over pressures for lowest common denominator schooling coming from international business interests remains to be seen.

* * *

One of the clearest signs of educational reform in post-apartheid South Africa is the proliferation of nongovernmental programs attempting, both formally and informally, to impact upon content and methodology. The most visible of these types of programs involve teacher training. From the creation of new textbooks, to the publication of teachers' stories and experiences, these often local projects have produced less controversy and perhaps more hope than the better-funded national campaigns. Though often based on the fundamental visions of the national policy makers and using the federal campaigns as a critical context, these grassroots efforts have achieved their successes largely because of their manageability: the practical nature of dealing with specific problems.

One of the most respected of the groups, the practitioners and scholars associated with the SACHED Trust, had a long-standing history in community work during the various apartheid regimes, publishing the work of the South African Democratic Teachers Union and the other progressive educational forces. As the transition from apartheid to democratic rule began, SACHED collected commentary from teachers about their new visions for education. The basic premise — that the policies of Christian National Education and Bantu Education (which prepared whites for power and Blacks for manual labor) were corrupt — seemed clear to all. As already documented, though, no unified vision on the local level existed (or exists) regarding exactly how to replace this system.[31]

A general area of interest for SACHED was the notion that the new school system could not simply "start afresh." There would have to be strategies for dealing with the "backlog" of apartheid. Two areas of some consensus and concern were the plight of the "ghetto" schools and of those students and community members most affected by the cruelties of a racist system. Jake, a lecturer at a teacher's training school in the large township of Soweto near Johannesburg, noted that "obviously all schools will be 'open' (integrated), but I believe that 'ghetto schools' with predominantly African students and unqualified teachers will be with us for at least the next twenty years."[32] Though model integrated schools may be produced, the majority of these township schools still had to be dealt with. Susan, a teacher in African and "Colored" as well as white schools in Cape Town, articulated the second concern: that many students will require special help in recovering from the violence and oppression of the previous system. "Many of our young people," she noted, "are traumatized by the past and will need help. Students will need help from trained remedial teachers and psychologists. We need more professionals who are trained to deal with specific problems to join the staffs of our schools."[33] Training of teachers and school officials takes place at one of several dozen loosely coordinated teachers' colleges throughout the country.

Most surveyed teachers agreed on the need for some unitary national system but had a variety of opinions on the need for centralization versus local control. SACHED in general noted that the tumultuous 1980s were a time of tremendous community participation in education, when groups like the United Democratic Front and the National Education Crisis Committee helped to set up alternative structures, as massive boycotts kept tens of thousands of students out of the formal school system. As the country was being made "ungovernable" under apartheid, local groups created their own makeshift schools based on democratic principles. Though many of the structures were temporary in nature and did not survive the shifts of the 1990s, some SACHED teachers suggest that one cannot simply wait for the new government programs or monies, but must build from the bottom up, re-forming student representative councils and parent-teacher-student associations.[34]

For those who worked and grew up in the shadow of a system as domineering and all-encompassing as apartheid, part of the job of these councils and associations had to be, especially for teachers, to provide acceptable space for self-criticism and, as some call it, action research.[35] With reflection on one's own history, education, and current teaching practice — both as individuals and, more importantly, in noncompetitive collegial groups — educators could "unlearn" the ways in which the old system influenced their pedagogy and learn new methods and modes. A teacher from an African school in KwaZulu, Phumzile, suggested that teachers must take the lead around questions of racism and ethnicity, using the schools and new curricula to bridge gaps between people and build a new, liberated nation. Soraya, a teacher in a nearby "Colored" school, added that a nonsexist approach must also be a special educational responsibility, in keeping with the strong antisexist guidelines of the new constitution.

Finally, the idea that teachers themselves — in conjunction with, in addition to, but ultimately separate from the various national and even schoolwide structures — must become agents for change, was reiterated by Thembi, a teacher at the Simon Hebe High School in the township of Mbakweri, outside Cape Town. Understanding that this would entail a great deal of consciousness and responsibility, Thembe stated: "Apart from what the schools choose to do as institutions, we must support teachers in [our] helping to develop a just educational system." Affirming this position, SACHED concluded that, with the commitment shared by so many local educators, the struggle to provide an antiracist, antisexist community and student-building education will ultimately be a "worthwhile and victorious one."[36]

That teaching under transformative circumstances is, in fact, a struggle is a point too often omitted from research and writings on alternative education. In the years following the election of Nelson Mandela, the Umlazi College for Further Education — and especially the in-service teacher-training Vulani Project — created an understanding of the need to struggle as a central theme of their work. Along with the Primary Open Learning Pathway Trust, a group also connected with SACHED, the Vulani Project published the seminal *Give Us Voices!* an educators' resource book adapted to the new country and conditions surrounding them. "Of the many challenges facing us," the authors began, "is the fact that three million children have been robbed the opportunity to dream....The dreams of a happy mind are the beginning of sophisticated thought processes."[37] Though the anthology covers a wide range of topics for both the new and the experienced teacher, the fundamental focus of the book is the advancement of literacy and numeracy across the subject areas, given both the new social circumstances and the limitation of federal resources. Though springing directly from the anti-apartheid and antiracist movements of South Africa, the Vulani leaders make clear that their ultimate concern is the development of democratic education throughout southern Africa and the entire continent.

Unsurprisingly, the Vulani group chose as their basic definition of literacy a two-sentence catch-all from Henry Giroux and Paulo Freire. "Literacy is the process," wrote Giroux and Freire, "whereby teachers, together with their pupils, gain the necessary knowledge to use their own insights to understand the world around them, so as to make constructive contributions to development and change in environments where resources are lacking or scarce. Literacy must be seen as a form of cultural production, giving children a strong sense of their own worth and creative ability and empowering them to transform oppressive conditions."[38] The authors at Vulani underscored the emphasis on process rather than end product and asserted that this definition has been selected because "it makes sense in the teaching and learning context of most teachers and pupils in southern Africa."[39] In fact, much of Freire's literacy education models were developed — after he was no longer "welcome" in his native Brazil — in the newly independent west African country of Guinea-Bissau. Some of the more practical lesson-planning sections of *Give Us Voices!* also suggest something of Frank Smith's influence. Smith, a U.S.-based literacy specialist famous for his assertions on the need to simplify the process of "reading without nonsense," also spent time evaluating the possibilities for educational reform in South Africa. Interviews with teachers play a role here again, as in this dialogue between teachers of African and European descent:

> NOMSA: Children learn to read by reading. The more children are guided through books and exposed to books, the more proficient they become at reading....If I had my way, my pupils would spend most of their time reading all kinds of books.
>
> PEGGY: Our teachers place far too much emphasis on the mechanics of reading (fluency, pronunciation, accent) and too little emphasis on the sense of reading (individual response, meaning, context).[40]

Student authorship, where teachers assist students in writing, developing, and publishing their own books — often for use in the classroom with their peers — is stressed as a key method for literacy. In Africa in particular, the use of elders in preserving on paper some of the oral traditions becomes an important and potentially motivating task for the current generation. Asking both students and teachers to use the community as a resource — to "find our words" (an adaptation of Freire) — they considered the transcription of oral history to paper as a means of building the "libraries of Africa," connecting children to their environment.

Their approach to dealing with the issues of racism and sexism raised by SACHED and others in the preceding years seemed particularly innovative. In addition to the assorted exercises common to U.S. multicultural programs, the Vulani Project suggested a checklist on teachers' attitudes, vis-à-vis "having an open mind." They listed a group of phrases almost every educator has said at one time or another and asked if that phrase was used or thought of "many times," "sometimes," or "never." Among the more challenging:

- I've tried that before.
- Our situation is different.
- That's not my job.
- I need more help.
- We've never done it before.
- We don't have the authority.
- We're not ready for that.
- Good idea, but impractical.
- It's never been tried before.
- We've always done it this way.[41]

Much of what Vulani and the Open Learning Pathway Trust collected was good, useful, and applicable to many situations and countries. Though not always South Africa-specific, one may assume, however, that their more subtle insights grew directly out of the difficulties encountered over the decades of divisiveness and oppression.

One more recent attempt at creating a postapartheid teacher-training manual, also put together by a well-respected, progressive publishing house, is Juta and Company's *The Courage to Lead: A Whole School Development Approach*, by Louise Sterling and Sue Davidoff. While filled with insightful anecdotes taken from field experiences over the last several years, the book in general provides less direction for the specific issues facing South Africa than most others covered in this report. Sterling and Davidoff work with the Teacher In-Service Project of the University of the Western Cape. Their focus is much more on the characteristics of "the leadership challenge" than on the elements of developing a "whole school" mentality. Aptly enough, they begin by noting the difficulties of reconstruction and change and by admitting: "For many of us involved in education, the context feels unstable. There is pressure from all sides which is felt most strongly at the point of delivery — the school. Socioeconomic conditions in South Africa," they continue, "impact on the school in many different ways." In addition to the demoralization and frustration of teachers, "few students can expect to be employed after they have completed their studies. This contributes to a feeling of despondency and demotivation among students, who often express their frustration through absenteeism, a lack of commitment to their own education, or other forms of negative behavior."[42]

The final point here, with all its poignant similarities to our own U.S. context, is nevertheless not significantly taken up by Sterling and Davidoff. In a listing that could only serve to remind one of the ingenious Vulani "open/closed mindedness" exercise, the Juta authors present an overwhelming list of teacher concerns, including:

- There is no long-term or inspirational vision.
- Staff in leadership positions lack competency.
- Leaders adhere rigidly to DOE dictates.
- Those in leadership show no accountability.

and adaptability, amazing things can happen and are happening in the provinces and among the grassroots.

* * *

Without a doubt, one of the most powerful campaigns in contemporary South Africa has been the movement for "truth and reconciliation" — for a way to accept and make reparations for the heinous history of apartheid while at the same time moving forward with hope, not recrimination. Much has been written about the official Truth and Reconciliation Commission (TRC), headed by Nobel Peace laureate Archbishop Desmond Tutu, and its attempts to forge a commonly agreed upon national consciousness about the abuses suffered under the racist regime while also creating a climate for healing. Tremendous international controversy surrounded most aspects of the TRC's work — from its attempts to get former President Botha to admit to his knowledge and endorsement of the criminal activity to the extensive questioning of Winnie Mandela for her part in the torture and murders of township youth accused of being "counter-revolutionary." Some complained that, with the possibility of amnesty for those who admit and disclose all their wrongdoings, the TRC traded justice in exchange for the truth. Still others felt that, with no judicial power (the TRC made recommendations to the government and was a moral rather than legal force), it could not come close to completing its mission.

The right wing bristled as it saw official history rewritten with them as the criminals; the idea that "a few rogue cops" were responsible for the primary injustices was cast aside. Average white South Africans had to come to terms with what apartheid meant for the majority. The liberation movements, on the other hand, were shocked that the TRC would condemn them, not for violence itself (there was no TRC consensus on pacifism per se), but for human rights abuses inflicted within their own ranks. That a group such as the TRC could stand above even Mandela and the anti-apartheid mainstream seemed unbelievable. In retrospect, however, one thing seems abundantly clear: the TRC

— despite much talk at the United Nations and South African constitutional level of the protection of human rights — the field of education has merely been able to explore options for recognition and respect. He is, however, forced to conclude that "the tensions in schools and the nonrecognition of our diverse culture have the potential of escalating into a full ethnic conflict."[48] In fact, Mda's summary of the confusions and conflicts relating to integration remains the strongest and most important indictment of all the "critical issues" facing teacher-trainers, administrators, and educators at the local level. "There appears to be a need for intervention," she notes, looking at the continued problems of racist attitudes despite the formal integration of schools, "especially by the government, through the Department of Education. It is, for instance, not enough to pass laws that are intended to transform and empower if there is no system for monitoring the process and ensuring implementation. A recent report on racism in desegregated high schools suggests that there is a crisis and it is a time bomb waiting to explode.[49] Meanwhile, Black learners and Black schools continue to be disadvantaged, and assimilation, rather than true integration in 'integrated' schools, is the order of the day."[50]

Despite these dire and important warnings, the Motshabi and the "kanniedood" schools, like the schools of Vulani's Nomsa and Peggy, prove that — on the local level — many exciting and innovative programs have developed in the postapartheid years. Though not in contradiction with the DOE's national campaigns, these examples appear to be based on a mixture of administration-teacher-student-community willingness to attempt innovation and work for change. As SACHED and Vulani demonstrate, there are lessons, approaches, and attitudes that all professionals within the educational system can use that will help make a school "exceptional." This survey of the graduate-level teacher and principal courses and colleges indicates that the problems facing education in South Africa today are larger even than mismanagement on the national ministry level. Long-term, countrywide solutions may be hard to pinpoint, but the prospects for hope are clear. With the proper vision, hard work, provided and continues to provide a great teachable moment in South Africa's history, where people are, formally and informally, reviewing their own pasts and discussing the nature of their collective future. From an educational perspective, the TRC is, in many ways, a greater space for transformative thinking and dialogue than the 1994 elections themselves — which no doubt made the TRC possible.

Dennis Brutus, one of South Africa's foremost poets and a former political prisoner on Robben Island with Nelson Mandela, has often pointed out that in 1995 he couldn't locate one white South African who admitted to ever being in favor of apartheid![51] By the late 1990s, after multiple hearings of the TRC, the debate focused primarily on who would take responsibility for apartheid and how a peaceful future would be constructed.

This author vividly remembers private meetings with Archbishop Tutu after the hearings had come to an end, as the commission was preparing to write its report. The archbishop was tired, worn out from the process of listening to extraordinary testimony of oppression, facilitating acts of forgiveness and conversation between perpetrators and victims, and pulling together commissioners from differing viewpoints into a coherent whole.[52] Our conversations were about a different but related topic — the uses and effects of nonviolence and armed struggle in the independence movements throughout Africa. Though these are often seen as tactical dichotomies, we discussed the need to look beyond the simplified "truths" to a sharper understanding of those ultimately struggling for a single goal: freedom and justice. In a book that grew out of these and other conversations, *Guns and Gandhi in Africa: Pan-Africanist Insights on Nonviolence, Armed Struggle and Liberation*, Tutu commented in his foreword that "Sutherland and Meyer have looked beyond the short-term strategies and tactics which too often divide progressive people. They have begun to develop a language which looks at the roots of our humanness beyond our many private contradictions."[53]

These "roots of our humanness" — the essence of what a postapartheid educational system would need to look for and at — have been much discussed by Archbishop Tutu and others. An

African principle has begun to enter widespread South African and international discourse, looking at the interconnectedness of people. *Ubuntu*, the "art of being human," the idea that one person's humanity is inextricably caught up in another's, is a socioeducational concept stemming from an indigenous, collective African worldview. In Xhosa, the proverb *"Umnto ngumntu ngabantu"* translates roughly to "I am because we are — we are because I am." Though ancient in the origins of the people of South Africa, its relevance remains striking. It speaks to the need for communality, human dignity, unity, pluralism, and multi-dimensionality. Compared to a more absolutist, monolithic, and individualistic European philosophical-education construct of "I think, therefore I am," *ubuntu* has begun to be taken up by South African educators and activists as a guiding force for interpreting and building on the present circumstances.

Nowhere is that work more thoroughly and forcefully laid out than in the writings of Maqhudeni Ivy Goduka. Her *Affirming Unity in Diversity in Education: Healing with Ubuntu* is a breathtaking analysis of the best of educational theory and practice internationally, applied to South African circumstances and supplemented with indigenous South African insights. Writing for and to all of South Africa's teachers, Goduka takes up the TRC challenge by suggesting that "the major questions for education as an institution and for educators and learners as individuals are not whether healing is necessary or whether it must take place in the classroom. The crucial questions are when, how and whether educators are ready to begin the calling to heal at different levels — that is, at the institutional, classroom and personal levels."[54] By presenting these questions as context, weaving together the personal and political, Goduka writes extensively on what "readiness" would look like and how it might be achieved.

Goduka begins her book by discussing the particular power of the personal narrative — how, by understanding and stating unapologetically who we are to others, we may transform a feeling and position of powerlessness into one of power. The narrative, in effect, becomes a personal first step in defining and asserting one's own humanness and therefore the place, as African American author Paula Giddings has termed it, "when and where I enter." One's narrative connects oneself with the rest of humanity.

As a model, Goduka presents her own narrative — full of consciousness and a strength of spirit — under the heading "You are now connecting with my voice and identities."[54] As a Xhosa woman with "geographic roots and cultural heritage" in Africa, educated under apartheid's Bantu educational system and then in a local Catholic school, she writes of multiple identities — born with, born into, some constructed, others imposed. Her political sophistication and sensitivity are easily recognized, for those interested in understanding them. For example, she writes that she was born heterosexual as an orientation, not as a sexual preference or choice. She writes of her gender, not as a given social construct, but as a biological indication based on her external and internal genitalia, hormones, and chromosomes. She writes specifically of the circumstances of family members who, under apartheid education, were taught to think differently than the *yobuntu* principles ingrained in African family life; aunts, uncles, grandparents living in one's home were no longer looked upon as part of the great whole but rather as part of some "other." When one African was hired to the faculty of an all-white school to teach an African language, no African students or white teachers took this as a serious act of change. Tokenism and separatism were hallmarks of the day.

Goduka reveals not just her own history, or even the history of the majority of African people or even the process by which one should or could write a narrative. Rather, her narrative serves to demonstrate a process whereby one may become ready to embrace *ubuntu*, to teach in such a way that affirms diversity, to become a member of a new society. She is clear at the outset, however, that there is never one "correct" way toward the *yobuntu* principle — not "one knowledge, one truth, one perspective, nor one center. Rather, knowledge or truth is politically, socially, culturally and historically constructed, deconstructed, reconstructed by different individuals at different times and from different centers, positions and perspectives. Knowledge," she explains, "can and should no longer be viewed as objective, value-free, neutral and apolitical."[55]

The preparation it takes to develop an education for healing and liberation, a transformative South African education, is not simply based on national priorities or curricula. An individual teacher can participate in and lead an effort for change, first, Goduka suggests, by clearing one's own "heart, mind, bones and soul" of racism and prejudices in the home as well as the self, in part through the narrative process. Secondly, there is an assertion that support groups are needed — within one's family, school, university, and community —to design and implement curricula and pedagogy and also to allow for the reality of making mistakes and moving forward. Lastly, and most difficult, one must form alliances with others who are working toward the elimination of oppression. Becoming an ally, Goduka notes, is very different (and more painful) than liberating oneself; it demands that one realize that there are no hierarchies of oppression and that all oppressions are linked to economic power and control. "When one becomes an ally," she poignantly observes, "one is constantly reminded that as long as we who are fighting oppression play the game of competition with one another, all forms of oppression will continue." As teachers, Goduka asserts, we must understand that "no one oppression can be eliminated without eliminating them all" and that elimination of oppressions in one's classroom can only succeed if one "replaces the assumptions of competition, hierarchy, and separation with the principle *yobuntu*."[57]

Before looking at the particularities of the South African situation, Goduka reviews the antibias work of U.S. educators Louise Derman-Sparks and James Banks, as well as the principles of *agape* and the Lakota *mitakuye oyasin* ("we are all related"). She adopts the most far-reaching multiculturalist approaches (as in Grant and Sletter's social reconstructionist model) and encourages South African educators to follow four guidelines to create an acceptable learning environment for unity in diversity. First, teachers should nurture each learner's construction of a knowledgeable, confident self-concept, cultural identity, and cultural voice. Second, teachers should promote each learner's comfortable, empathic interaction with people from diverse backgrounds. Third, educators must foster each learner's critical thinking about bias. Finally, the responsibility of the educator is to cultivate each learner's ability to defend self and others in the face of discrimination.[58] This proactive system assumes that all educators must first (and continually) face their own and their colleagues' values, experiences, biases, and "asymmetrical" positions of power in society and in the classroom.

Peace education is also reviewed and adapted, as part of an antibias and affirmative educational transformation. Though the word "peace" is common in almost all languages, its daily experience and practice is far from clearly understood. Goduka again looks at the work of U.S. leaders in the field, such as that of Betty Reardon, and brings the work into a South African context. Calling to mind the writings of Dr. Martin Luther King, Jr., and the work of the U.S. civil rights movement, she states that "the difference between peace as the absence of war and peace as the achievement of tranquility and harmony calls to mind the difference between desegregation of South African schools and their integration in recent years."[59] To integrate must mean more than that different ethnic groups are no longer separated on the attendance rolls, but rather that there exists understanding, mutual respect, beneficial interactions, and the presence of justice. Similarly, in an affirmative concept of peace, the validation of diversity — the teaching of *ubuntu* — is a prerequisite. Nonviolence, not as the opposite of armed struggle but rather as the presence of strategies for conflict prevention, negotiation, arbitration, mediation, and power sharing, is a key part of this affirmative peace education. In Goduka's words, echoing Gandhi and all the strategic advocates of a practical and revolutionary nonviolence, "conflict is a normal, natural human process. In a diverse society and in inclusive classrooms it is inevitable. It can be constructive or destructive, depending on how it is handled."[60] Constructive conflict, not yet learned by the nation-states of any political ideology or economic predisposition, nor truly desired by those who hold the reins of power and privilege in any society, may be possible in a classroom context with an agreed upon understanding of our interconnectedness and humanness.

Goduka cleverly turns the terminology of disadvantaged and privileged classrooms and schools on its head. Asserting that *Affirming Unity in Diversity in Education* is not simply for those who have been marginalized by Eurocentric curricula and apartheid, she suggests that transformative education "seeks to empower all learners by instilling in them the principles and spiritual values that are required to begin healing, and which are necessary for survival in South Africa's culturally and socially diverse society."[61] Anyone lacking the skills to thrive in a diverse society, including the skills associated with the *yobuntu* principle, should therefore be considered disadvantaged.

This plays out in a very particular way with regard to language as a transmitter of culture. If language is both a fundamental sign of humanity and inextricably linked to culture, then the languages that are (or are not) taught in school become significant in building a new society. In South Africa, English is the lingua franca between people with different mother tongues, but isi Zulu, isi Ndebele, isi Xhosa, Tshivenda, Xitsonga, Afrikaans, and other languages are spoken in the homes of the majority of the people. Studies have shown that multilingual children develop a certain "cognitive flexibility," or ability to think about divergent issues, in a manner more sophisticated than monolingual learners. Contact with and respect for "family values" may also play a role. Goduka notes that in the U.S., Cuban American students have the highest educational levels of all Latinos and are also the most likely to speak Spanish at home. Mono-lingualism, even if the language one speaks is the dominant English, becomes a sign of a disadvantaged education.

Finally, Goduka reviews the South Africa Office of Population Census (OPC) wording regarding people with physical "disabilities." The OPC survey asks, "Are your difficulties in understanding people mainly due to a hearing problem?" as opposed to "Are your difficulties in understanding people mainly due to their inability to communicate with you?" OPC questioned students: "Have you attended a special school because of a long-term health problem or disability?" rather than: "Have you attended a special school because of your education authority's policy of sending people with your health problem or disability to such places?" The emphasis becomes clear. When OPC simply asks, "Can you tell me what is wrong with you?" Goduka's rewording should be easily anticipated: "Can you tell me what is wrong with society?"[62]

Significantly, Maqhudeni Ivy Goduka does not comment extensively on the national DOE policies, Curriculum 2005, or the controversies of OBET. Though mentioning them all at one point or another, she fundamentally suggests that there is no contradiction between "healing with *ubuntu*" and any of those policies. Implicit, however, is the idea that a review of and incorporation of the principle *yobuntu* is more fundamental to educational and social change (or to social change through transformative education) than these other initiatives. She states that, as provinces have been given the responsibility for developing and implementing their own policies at different levels, the responsibility of the teacher is to "advance beyond formal proclamations in their pursuit of the cause to educate all learners in an environment that affirms and validates their unity as human beings, yet affirms and validates the unique and special gifts that each learner brings to the classroom."[63]

Perhaps beyond *ubuntu* itself, Goduka's own unique mix of the best of Euro-American transformative educational philosophy and African social philosophy makes her arguments about the future of South Africa so compelling. She is certainly not the most well known or noted educational theorist or practitioner on the continent — or, for that matter, in the U.S., where she taught at Central Michigan University. Her grasp, nonetheless, of Cummins, Gardner, the Sadkers, Cornel West, and others already mentioned and her ability to "translate" Western educational concepts to South African circumstances suggest a special skill and insight into what may be needed to build the future we all appear to be looking for. Like the Pan-Africanist principles discussed previously, *yobuntu* and democracy comingle as precepts for a liberating school, home, and society. Goduka concludes her vital study noting that "these principles cannot be taught didactically; they must be caught. For learners to catch these principles, they must live with them, by them and observe them modeled or enacted by significant adults....They must understand the importance of politics, debate, social action and the acquisition of power...and acquire skills for nonviolent conflict resolution."[64]

The South African national school system may not yet be at that point of achievement, where these principles are molded together and put into practice. Goduka, however, is not the only one who makes clear that these goals are being talked about, debated, and in some circumstances implemented. In local projects, individual classrooms, and regional initiatives, there are unquestionably growing spaces for new thinking and educational change. In some places, such as the Cape Town–based Quaker Peace Center, the education is conducted informally through community organizations.[65] In other places, projects such as Vulani or the SACHED initiatives train teachers formally to broaden their scope. In a society that has, in less than ten years, gone through extraordinary turmoil and national change, there are so many contradictions that appear crazy from one angle, inevitable from another. The globe's longest-held political prisoner is released and becomes the globe's most respected president. A leader of the Communist Party of South Africa also attends Quaker meetings; an avowed antimilitarist, she becomes deputy minister of defense.[66] When walking through the offices of the TRC, this author noticed a staff photo of a familiar face: Zenzile Xhosian, a journalist in exile in New York throughout the 1980s had returned home to South Africa and joined the TRC investigative staff. He spent the latter part of the 1990s going to the police stations that had once hunted him, now demanding that they unlock their secret files and hand them over for review.[67]

* * *

When Kader Asmal was appointed South African Minister of Education, it was at a point when some school districts — in an effort to create a "color-blind" attitude — were labeled by some as attempting to "erase history." That a major liberation movement leader such as Steve Biko would be unknown and untaught even in predominantly Black regions was offset by the fact that Asmal, a former history instructor himself, quickly developed a broad-ranging national "South African History Project" to attempt to address the "realities of the past." That the project was headed up by June Bam, a prominent critic of early governmental policies, was taken by many as a promising sign that more intensive and comprehensive initiatives would soon be under way.[68]

Indeed, the DOE's own self-evaluation of the changes in policy from 1994 to 2001 included some sober assessment of the precarious tightrope South African national policy was attempting to walk. "We took a conscious decision," noted Asmal, "to understand the emerging form and function of globalization, and locate our country as a competitive economy within this context."[69] With the globalized erosion of the political importance of the nation-state, however, South Africa asserted its national interests and identity, attempting to counter, at least on a symbolic level, the homogenization of governments and business. South Africa, Asmal asserted, set out against the general tide of globalized academics to stay true to a commitment regarding the responsibility of the government to provide lifelong education and care for its people.

Within this context, the DOE suggested that 2001-2002 was a period moving "from action to institutionalization," where basic school functionality increased and provincial education systems were better able to manage fiscal and human resources. A clearer focus on delivery and implementation was evident at this time.[70] Most notably, a National Qualifications Framework Structure (NQFS) was put into effect, seeking to bring together "education and training skills development [for] the needs of critical democracy."[71] Drawing on lessons from popular campaigns, including the People's Education Movement and the Congress of South African Trade Unions' vocational education models, NQF attempted to incorporate flexibility, a recognition of both formal and informal learning, and a "portability of credentials" with the clear need for a nationally regulated set of basic standards.

By the end of 2001, the DOE convened a conference, including international representatives, on "Values, Education, and Democracy in the 21st Century." Far from drawing on the massive educational and statistical data and conditional support available from groups such as the World Bank, the 2001 conference brought together radical and critical educators of the contemporary scene. Palestinian intellectual and Columbia University professor Edward Said implored attendees to remember that a thinking and active population can only be achieved through a "mobilized, criticized, and secular understanding of humanistic book-based education, that is, reading literature."[72] john powell, U.S. director of the Institute on Race and Poverty, called for a deep and broad examination of the continuing role of race and racism in both South Africa and the U.S., noting that a "transformative action policy" must still be developed on the institutional, communal, and personal levels.[73]

A forward-looking set of policies for South African education must be based on a clear and partisan political assessment of what takes place in the real-world classroom. The chair of the review committee for Curriculum 2005, Linda Chisholm, honestly stated that the loose and teacher-based system of selection of content allowed equally for a strong antiracist curriculum ...or a racist one! Current initiatives, therefore, place strong emphasis on guidelines based explicitly on human rights, inclusivity, and social justice.[74] And Pan-African solidarity focusing on aid to townships and rural schools, most notably through the building of Schools of Leadership targeting poor girls and funded by a U.S.$20 million grant from Oprah Winfrey, has brought the need to confront continuing economic injustices to a world audience. Former University of Natal deputy vice chancellor Ahmed Bawa, now a program officer for the Ford Foundation, has written of the positive collaborations being built between academic universities and workers' training colleges. "At the time when South African higher education is attempting to reinvent itself," Bawa wrote, "it must see itself as the key institution for nurturing a broad intellectual culture."[75] In many ways, it is still too soon to tell whether these guidelines, partnerships, and newly strengthened national priorities will be able to see to the implementation of the broad and lofty early goals of progressive educational change.

These goals, in any case, have continued to be reiterated at the national level. Despite the fact that a major initiative on

Race and Values was a latecomer to the official priorities of the DOE's Tirisano Plan, it is noteworthy that a key national report was concluded with a renewed call for education for all, quoting none other than Vietnamese communist leader Ho Chi Minh. "An ignorant nation is a weak nation," wrote Ho. Illiteracy is "an enemy as dangerous as foreign aggression and famine."[76]

Transformation continues to take place in South Africa on a widespread basis. More change is certainly needed. For transformation to take place thoroughly within the field of education, greater resources and intensified commitment are certainly still needed. Today, *ubuntu*, an understanding of one's humanness, is no longer a strange and closeted Xhosa superstition. *Ubuntu*'s power, as well as its beauty and vitality, is that it can and must start with the commitment of one.

Chapter 7

ERITREA AT TEN: VICTORIES AND REALITIES

Eritrea at ten was a mixture of somber reflection and unbridled celebration. The spectacular midnight fireworks that lit up Asmara's sky to usher in the May 24 activities were barely as exciting as the looks on the faces of the throngs of thousands simply milling about on the main street — greeting and embracing old friends and comrades. The street, once off limits to all but the colonial elite in the days before independence, was packed so tightly that a native New Yorker could feel right at home, as in a crowded evening's rush-hour subway commute. A marked difference here, however, was the comfort of safety. No robberies or fights, no thefts or acts of violence were about to erupt. This was the space of freedom, full of smiles. Strolling down the street was an act of pride, affirmation, and joy, with spontaneous outbursts of dancing or singing and only an occasional uneasy pondering of a still uncertain future.

May 2001 marked not simply the tenth anniversary of the EPLF takeover of the capital, the driving out of the Ethiopian military and administrative forces, or the eighth anniversary of the referendum that ensured full independence and international recognition. It also signified the six-month mark since the signing of a new peace treaty with Ethiopia, one that sought to end a three-year border dispute that cost close to 70,000 lives. The renewed war was a shock to many inside and out of the country, in part because of its intensity and in part because, more than any other recent policy, it symbolized an uneasy disjuncture between the mainstream of Eritrean society and its normally beloved leadership.

A difficult maturation of the Eritrean people, movement, and nation has taken place over the last several years, with the mystique of the liberation fighters — those who led the thirty-year war — greatly diminished. Massive numbers of young people have experienced at least some time "at the front," and the entire country is filled both with a sense of "ownership" — of having defended their homeland — and of exhaustion at the very concept of war. President Isais Afwerki, towering over those of us seated in the VIP section of the national stadium on May 24, admitted that the war "meant the stagnation and regression of [Eritrea's] economic growth and national development"[1] — including the priority of education for all. Though still respected, Afwerki came under an unprecedented amount of open criticism and questioning, both concerning his handling of the war and of the undemocratic and disorganized nature of the government. Much has been aired about the lack of services and programs provided to the population, even before the onset of the 1998 crisis. While these very criticisms, voiced in the newspapers, by cabinet members, and among the "intelligentsia," indicated a dynamic democratic commitment and involvement, they sadly also reflected an Eritrea that had not made the gains many had hoped for ten years prior or during the thirty-year war.

Viewing the packed stadium from just behind the presidential and ministerial section, one could not help but get caught up in the energy and excitement of the hundreds of youth and students who participated in a ninety-minute multimedia show, reflecting Eritrea's hopes and vision. Significantly, the celebration was marked not with the speeches of multiple politicians — only the president made a formal presentation — but by the songs, dances, dress, and drama of the nine ethnic groups that make up the country. After months of practice, the youth put on a theatrical pageant that rivaled Broadway's best, with special effects, banners, and expertly coordinated placards displayed by students sitting in the audience. The story of Eritrea was told in an accessible and inspiring form, and that fact alone created space in one's heart and mind for thinking positively about the future. As I traveled the country in the days following May 24, and the official celebration was rebroadcast in public places and private homes throughout the land, I sought to find out what else occupied the thoughts of youth, students, and those involved in their education.

* * *

On the official level, plans for education in Eritrea postindependence have been articulated in several media. Gebre Hiwet Tesfagiorgis, editor of *Emergent Eritrea: Challenges of Economic Development*, wrote clearly of education as the "main ingredient" of human resources and socioeconomic development, noting — as many other Eritrean leaders have stated — that education and national education goals must be an integral part of a national development plan.[2] Stating that education, in general, is an "expensive but worthwhile investment" in the nation's future, he asserted that education and equity must be the state's responsibility, with five top goals to keep in mind. Tesfagiorgis recommended that full functional literacy be achieved by 2005; that free, compulsory, universal primary education be in place for all by 2000; that Eritrean cultures be promoted within the educational system to foster equality and unity among the country's diverse peoples; that general education be combined with technical/vocational education to meet the nation's development needs; and that a center of basic and applied research be created so that higher education could train people who would then provide various specialized services throughout Eritrea. This five-point plan, fundamental as far as the Revolution Schools principles of the 1980s were concerned, was also clearly ambitious. Tesfagiorgis admitted that adult and informal educational activities, taking place beyond the walls of any classroom or schoolhouse, would be needed to supplement the state programs and achieve any of the five policies.[3]

In the area of secondary school education, there is another admission inherent in the five-goal plan: that resource constraints do not allow for universal high school education. Therefore, the pressures on those who are able to attend high school are ever more intense, as are the pressures on secondary school teachers to make their work relevant. In *Emergent Eritrea*, Yegin Habtes suggested that as Eritrea approached the year 2000, high school education might not be "sufficient." Specialized vocational secondary schools that focused on narrow, "hands-on" experiences but with little intellectual substance would leave Eritrea with a long-term gap. "Specialized vocational schools," Habtes wrote, "should provide their graduates with the knowledge and skills that they need for work and the pursuit of higher education."[4]

One key component of policy articulation and implementation — for relevant teaching in all schools at all levels — is the production of meaningful curricula. Joan Sullivan-Owomoyela worked with the Curriculum Institute and with the Ministry of Education (MOE) from 1993 until 1996, focusing much attention on how Eritrean indigenous systems could be utilized to make the national curriculum and ministry work as relevant as possible. The MOE, she noted, spent much of the early postindependence period "undertaking an extensive national curriculum review to improve the quality of education" and make the school system reflect people's local as well as national needs. By examining indigenous precolonial African learning styles and modes, she suggested, implications could be drawn to take practical knowledge and make it reinforced and structured into the formal academic environment.[5]

Creating a framework for the categorization and adaptation of indigenous educational techniques, Sullivan-Owomoyela's research began with the premise that indigenous education "prepares an individual to accommodate and create changes in his/her community."[6] This premise also implied that people who are "physically and culturally accessible" as well as "economically viable" to their communities may be better prepared by incorporating indigenous "integrative and integral systems." In Eritrea in particular, "threads of commonality" between the nine ethnic groups were espoused, allowing for holistic curricular possibilities. Cultural competencies were identified for the indigenous education framework, with special emphasis on fine arts, linguistics, logical reasoning, and interpersonal relationships.

In the all-important area of linguistics and primary-language acquisition — so essential for basic literacy and empowerment — a comparison of how the ethnic groups describe children was conducted. The more literal Tigrinya call their youngsters *endu* (small one), which has both descriptive and affectionate connotations. Both boys and girls among the Kunama are referred to as *fasha* (good) or *fadaba* (nice), while the Tigre nationality demonstrably prioritizes the child's role, referring to children as *sray* (medicine for one's soul). In Saho culture, male children are afforded more respect, as boys may be referred to as *lubak* (lion, or courageous), but girls cannot.[7] Each of these examples suggests how an Eritrean subgroup socializes its youth. An indigenous education competencies framework could explore, through curricular reform, how formal schools could use this information to adapt literacy "situations" to the culture of the child or the child's cultural background to a given literacy objective. While much of this cultural sensitivity vis-à-vis literacy and linguistics in particular has been a fundamental component of Eritrean education, much has been written about what still needs to be done and what a truly multilingual society will look like, with English, Arabic, Tigrinya, a local language (for non-Tigrinya speakers), and Italian (for older Eritreans) all in conversational use. There is fairly widespread agreement, amidst various debates, that Eritrea's continuing commitment to indigenous language development is one of its education system's strongest achievements.[8]

In the area of interpersonal relationship competencies, Sullivan-Owomoyela explained the *baito* system, whereby every village or town has a representative elected by the people to represent them within the community government structures. This legal mandate within Eritrea not only provides for the possibility of truly democratic institutions, but also utilizes long-existing indigenous decision-making processes. Few better lessons or models for the relevance of education on the local level (civics, if you will) can be manufactured by any outside national or international bodies. Not every Eritrean ethnic grouping, after decades of war, has a fully intact trial elder system, but respecting these systems where they do exist and attempting to strengthen them where they are weak provide a tremendous lesson about the connectedness of schooling and social involvement.[9] The MOE studies cited and worked on by Sullivan-Owomoyela and others designed a "Test for Multiple Competencies" — an alternative assessment/multiple intelligence derivative — which was used to show educational planners how to make these connections as obvious and teachable as possible. "An understanding of how people learn in their indigenous societies," she concluded, "enables the roles of teacher and learner to be harmonized in a more formal learning environment, and permits a transference between practical [indigenous] and academic [formal] knowledge."[10]

Another prominent practitioner, dean of the Faculty of Education at the University of Asmara, Dr. Belainesh Araya, emphasized a different set of deep-seated challenges facing those who work with contemporary Eritrean youth. In *Counseling in an Eritrean Context*, Araya noted that traditional family bonds in Eritrean culture are "multigenerational and enormously strong."[11] Asserting that there is a great emphasis on preserving harmony between past and present and that identity is derived from one's connection to family (as opposed to the Western identification with one's accomplishments), Araya explains that an often unquestioning obedience to elders can complicate students' relationships to teachers or clinicians. "It is safe to state that one of the developmental tasks for young Eritreans," Araya writes, "is navigating their way through the many social, cultural/traditional, environmental, and economic challenges facing their nation."[12] The role of educators is to understand these developmental pressures and to create schools that are appropriately geared toward supporting students who may then support Eritrea itself.

* * *

The Eritrean Ministry of Education is prominently located in the capital on the main street itself, near the central post office. During May 2001, a neighboring café had an eight-foot-high papier-mache fist in the front, with flags flying amidst the national slogan, "Victory to the Masses." In front of the Ministry itself were groupings of students throughout the day. Some were selling tenth anniversary T-shirts as fund-raisers; others — art students — were involved in a project whereby folks off the street would take some paints and a one-foot-square area of canvas to produce a message for posterity. The mural of individual messages would be preserved and displayed at various future functions. One of the young women cajoled me into taking brush in hand. I drew a heart, another national symbol, and wrote the word "solidarity," while a friend penned in Tigrinya a rough transliteration: "*Hade Lebi*," one heart.

Inside the Ministry, a computer-filled office serves as the central Bureau of Statistics. Here, rhetoric serves little purpose; numbers are crunched and evaluations are made on areas of progress or stagnation. The MOE annual reports, unlike those of South Africa, have no pronouncements or predictions. They are simply a series of charts, with a single-page executive summary to review the major trends. Statistics are broken down according to geographic region, ages and genders of students, grade enrollment figures, teachers available per school and region, numbers of special education students or grade repeaters, languages of instruction used (with twenty subcategories of languages/groups), physical facilities (i.e., classrooms, toilets) available, participation rates, tests passed, and more. In most areas, numbers are given for the current year as well as the previous years since independence. The ability to compare and contrast, to draw interpretations and conclusions, is left open to the skills or desires of the reader. The reports, though dense, are impressive; they deliver important information in hard and clear figures.

One need only look at a single page to get a sense of the direction of the system. A table, for example, on population and net enrollment in secondary schools showed that from 1991 to 1999 there had been a slow but steady annual increase in school participation for both males and females. And while male enrollment for fourteen- to seventeen-year-olds has consistently been higher every year than that of their female counterparts, the percentage growth rate of enrollment increase for females has been greater over the eight-year period surveyed. Thus, by the end of 1999, male percentage enrollment in high school was up from 8.6 percent to 12.6 percent, and female enrollment increased from 8.3 percent to 10.0 percent.[13] When one looks at total population figures, this is still a far cry from universal secondary education, but it indicates steps in the right direction. The rate of school repeaters over this same period had decreased substantially, from 29.7 percent to 9.4 percent for males and from 51.2 percent to 17.6 percent for females.

Looking at statistics for 2001, still in preliminary form as the MOE took pains to review and reconfirm their figures, elementary school education enrollment on the whole increased to 13 percent throughout the country. Though open to a variety of interpretations, this fundamentally suggests that a very high percentage of school-age children from five to ten years old are receiving at least basic literacy and math instruction. The executive summary admits that "due to the amplified population estimate," the increase was lower than originally hoped for. Nonetheless, all numbers are up, a special emphasis on examining the participation of girls is noteworthy, and adult literacy programs, even during wartime, increased enrollment by 130 percent. The number of literacy program centers created is reputed to have increased by an incredible 267 percent![14] Numbers, of course, do not tell the whole story, and for North American educators suspicious of statistics — which have too often been used against progressive causes — we may believe that anecdotal evidence counts more than numerical indicators. Tools, however, when used as such, can provide one window into a larger picture. To peer at the question from another perspective, I began at the grassroots.

* * *

"The policies of the Ministry of Education are written in pencil," said eleventh-grader Kessete from Grad Fesuh in central Eritrea. "They are changing and changing all the time." An average student, now completing his studies in Asmara, Kessete has been working hard all his life, leading up to a moment about to take place some weeks after our chat over tea, just by the central market. Two of his friends have joined us, but neither of them awaits the school-leaving tests that will determine Kassete's future. If he's in the top 4 or 5 percent of his class, he'll have a possibility of admission to the University of Asmara and higher education in general. If not, perhaps he can go back to his village and survive on subsistence farming or working with family and relatives. "Right now," he reflects, "I don't even feel qualified to hold up a pen or paper."

Tsehaye, a tall, quiet type from Adi Kolan, has already begun specialized postgraduate study at the private Don Bosco Technical Training School in Dekemhare, a small but vibrant town some thirty minutes from the capital. "Where are the good teachers now?" he asked, thinking back over his year in the public schools. "There is not enough money, there are not enough teachers for the courses, there are not enough materials like labs for science. So many teachers and students have become demoralized." In the higher grades, Tsehaye suggested, students have no choice but to focus all attention on the exams, also a demoralizing dynamic. "Even if I am very clever, the university cannot tolerate a high percentage" of smart students. More secondary schools must be built.

"More universities as well!" chimed in Solomon, a tenth grader from Jeretuwa, also studying in Asmara. A year away from the critical examinations, with a personality more focused on sociability than on academic concerns, Solomon was one of a number of students mistakenly taken into military training during the three-year war. When questioned about the time at "boot camp" anticipating possible deployment to the front lines, Solomon spoke of how many people he knew already serving. "Even my father, all our parents and brothers are at the front," he stated. "We were not afraid to die at the time....If we would have shown fear of being killed, there would be more chance of attack." What he did describe as "horrible" was his loss of time at school. "We were worried about our studies," he noted, "so some of us wanted to return."

"When the war broke out," Tsehaye admitted, "I was completely demoralized. There was a real question facing all of us: Are we going to live or to die?"

On a more forward-looking note, Kessete spoke of his own hopes for possible educational reform. "If I were to speak with the minister of education," he suggested, "I would tell him to organize more meetings with students and ask about our problems, especially in the high schools. We did have one meeting," he recalls, "with teachers and administrators," but more talk is needed about the limitations facing students interested in college education. In addition to involving students in the problem-solving process of school and social change, clearly the recent war left its effects on all students. "Clever, educated teachers should not be sent to the front," Kessete recommended. And finally, a more universal cry: "We should be given more tolerant and competent teachers."[15]

Father Angelo Regazzo, the founder and director of the Don Bosco Technical Training School, sympathized with the perspectives set forth by the students interviewed. A European Catholic educator, trained in various Asian schools, Regazzo has followed the general mission of the Don Bosco order in building schools that can teach practical trades. Providing students not necessarily going to university with a chance for a certificate in generalized study, the school teaches vocational skills so that students can find paying jobs upon graduation. The Eritrean government supports these efforts politically and fiscally, and they undoubtedly take some of the burden off of the tightly squeezed public system. With a high demand for teachers and schools and a shortage of supply, the MOE currently depends on collaborations such as the one with Don Bosco, but in some ways these technical training schools have, in themselves, become centers servicing an intellectual elite.

Regazzo sighed at the thought of the complex situation both he and the MOE are in. Everyone wants to provide education for all, with expert specialization but also a general base of critical and practical knowledge. He bounced us around at a frantic pace, from woodshop to computer lab to garden, talking of how all the desks and tables are constructed by Don Bosco students and how a few more chickens in the farm area could provide a model for self-sufficiency, with enough eggs for a hearty daily breakfast for all learners. Ultimately, however, Regazzo could not help but come back to his basic philosophy: "Our purpose here is to reach the poor." With little if any tone of condescension, he suggested that a university education should not be looked upon as the be-all and end-all in a largely rural society on a largely rural planet. "The more you get away from the poor, the more you want to work behind a desk wearing a tie, the more problems you will have solving your own problems — and solving the problems of this country," he stated. Talking like a true liberation theologian — or like the Catholic Worker educators of our own country — Regazzo soulfully engaged us: "If we form people who are afraid to dirty their hands, we will all be in trouble."[16]

* * *

In a tiny but popular bar near downtown Asmara, tables were filling up in the predinner rush on independence eve. With a four-day weekend to commemorate the tenth anniversary, folks were coming into the capital from many surrounding areas. It was there that two Mendefera-based math teachers began to narrate — before drinks — their complaints and concerns.

"Seventy to eighty students in one class," Dawit insisted, "cannot stay interested in the subject matter. There is a positive vision for education in this country, but it won't come to pass for another ten years." With an extreme shortage of teachers and a salary that does not encourage graduates to go into the profession, the current prospects, despite statistics, are quite bleak.

"There is a program I'm a part of," explained Hailemariam, who teaches with Dawit at St. Georgio/Adi Ugri, "to send teachers like myself for training overseas. For two years, we get extensive experience in London or in the schools of South Africa and can come back with positions reflecting our greater understanding of curriculum development, instructional media, and so forth." This reliance on outside forces undoubtedly influences more than just educational or methodological practices. Believing that middle and secondary education should be taught in English only, Hailemariam demonstrated a cultural predisposition that is becoming common and seen as more practical. "Tigrinya, as a subject, would be good. But as part of a bilingual program — not everything need be done this way. English is used in the university and in foreign settings, so should be used early on here."

"The reason it will take ten years to reach our vision," continued Dawit, "is because of all the problems we currently face. Teachers should only teach one shift a day and a maximum twenty-four-hour-a-week instructional block, instead of the current thirty-six hours. There should be a maximum of forty students per class. We need to build more schools and recruit more teachers. Most of all, our salaries must be increased, above those workers serving other ministries. To be fully solved, this problem of teacher shortage must see to a doubling of the current number of educators — up to at least seven thousand."

Both teachers suggested that, while strides were being made in the area of gender equity, with special government-supported after-school and weekend classes for girls, the move toward democratization was slow to nonexistent. "We are definitely not given a role in shaping what school policy is like," noted Dawit. "The Teachers Association," added Hailemariam, is a union "in name only. It has not been useful at all." Additional recommendations for reforms included: giving houses or accommodations to all teachers, especially those sent somewhere outside of where they originally lived; instituting evening classes for failing students; and focusing more attention on rural communities, whose youth have to simultaneously serve as farmers as well as students. Parents and community members in all parts of the country, they admitted, are beginning to get involved through cooperation and school-based collaboration. Education is seen as vital, but few teachers — including Dawit and Hailemariam — seemed prepared to incorporate the lessons of nonformal, "uneducated" elders into the basics of day-to-day study.[17]

At first I must admit to being somewhat shocked at the negativity and apparent pessimism of these teachers from Mendefera. There was clearly a wide gap between their thoughts and experiences on the one hand, and the general impression of Eritrea's educational successes on the other. As it became clear that they were, in fact, representative of many community-based educators, especially at the secondary school level, it seemed necessary to look more closely at how the years between 1996 and the present had affected the school system nationally. An appointment was set up for an interview with writer-historian Alemseged Tesfai, one of Eritrea's leading intellectuals and a consultant throughout the years with several ministries and educational initiatives.

Arriving early for our meeting at his meager office in the building of the Eritrean Research and Documentation Center, Alemseged was ready to see us at 8 a.m. as we arrived.[18] His salt-and-pepper beard and gentle smile belie his many years and many roles in the struggle, at one point heading up the Eritrean Land Commission, now primarily working on an authoritative documentary of the independence movement. "I was at the beginning of the educational process of the EPLF," he began directly, "one of the founders of the Zero/Revolution School and chair of the curriculum committee. Some of us were teachers, with experience and degrees from teacher-training institutes, but I was a lawyer by trade, never thinking that I'd be part of an educational structure.

"The philosophy of education at the beginning," he continued, "was based upon two distinct principles. First, we felt that education had to be as practical as possible....had to be a link to practice itself and to the realities and needs of the environment facing the country. Secondly, we were committed to the idea that education should always be taught in the mother tongue, at least through primary school level."

Alemseged recounted how the EPLF tried to put their principles into practice, developing and preparing special curriculum and language texts, dealing specifically with issues involving the revolution. He frankly stated that the language aspect of their principles were always problematic and still are. The emphasis on Arabic by some was attacked as having overly religious motivations in a secular state and struggle, but now Eritreans have come back with doctorates from Egypt or other parts of the Middle East and have difficulty working in primarily English-language or Tigrinya-dominated offices. Professional development and Eritrea's ability to train its own people and develop its own materials within a multilingual context are pivotal to the long-term resolution of this conflict. Otherwise, one can infer a split between the largely illiterate rural communities who would benefit most from mother-tongue instruction and the highly educated urban leadership, who might appropriately need one (or at most two) uniformly acceptable languages of communication and documentation.

When asked about the apparent gap between the educational ideals of the EPLF and the current problems facing teachers and many students, Alemseged reflected again on the early days. "At the Revolution School, we knew that we were lagging behind. We had a whole generation of people in the 1970s and '80s who were not at all educated but were committed to the country." The process of both education and teacher training at the school was very personalized, intensively hands-on and community-specific, with a highly motivated group of learners. "The kids that were brought up in that school," he said with quiet pride, "are some of the best teachers we have in this country. They have stuck firmly to our original desires."

In general, Alemseged continued, educational policy and practice has been one of Eritrea's major successes, with the most obvious indication of this being the building of new schools. "The government boasts of being countryside-friendly," he noted, "and in the practice of building schools, one can see that this makes it true." The level of education in most urban areas, he admitted, leaves much to be desired. "There are too few schools, too many students per class, students not getting a proper education, and teachers getting increasingly frustrated.... We're stuck with people who think that they're educated but they're not." Without giving a clear indication of where to place the blame or how to pinpoint the roots and solutions to this problem, Alemseged stated with a certain sadness, "It has taken a long time to begin to deal with these issues....This unhealthy cycle must be broken."[19]

* * *

"Any country which starts from scratch in education," noted Dr. Hailemikael Mesgina sympathetically, "must first and foremost deal with the numbers. They don't deal with the quality. I grant you that quality of education is not what it should be, but that's the next stage of the struggle."[20]

In Mesgina's living room, one is surrounded by the artifacts and colors of a lifetime in service to the people of Africa and the world. Sculptures from every part of the continent line one row atop a bookshelf, while baskets woven by every ethnic group within Eritrea lie on a tabletop. Mesgina's decades of work at UNESCO, eventually as the chief of their Africa programs, as well as his current consultantship with Eritrea's MOE and his own Cultural Heritage Project are reflected in his humble but well-decorated home. We speak of problems and solutions, without any sense of propriety or holding back.

"I see the flaws, but I also see the other side of the coin," he continued. "The government doesn't have the resources. It's not realistic that it can do all things at once. Communities are worried about the quality of education: science education, books, insufficient libraries, poor administration, and the quality of educational opportunities. I am also worried: how can a teacher deal with sixty children and also deal with the problems of a few?

"At the same time, the government is trying to spread the quantity of education — up to grade five — to everyone throughout the country. In the next stage, after having spread education to all, in their own languages, with their own textbooks, we take a closer look at quality. The MOE is, itself, worried....I think personally that they have to improve science education, using it to develop critical thinking skills, doubting, asking for evidence. Also, we don't have sufficient language teaching. Our English-language education is a mess, with teachers who are not well trained at all. In a transition time like this one, we've got to use technology — radio and cassettes — to teach English to many people at once and closed-circuit television to teach some basics of science.

"The minister of education asked me what to do. I suggested two priorities that we have to develop. First, there must be intensified teacher training. If a nation has good teachers, then it has good citizens. Secondly, there must be expanded technical education: a two-level system whereby school leavers have several choices aside from simply going to university or being told that you can't go on. This has a tremendous negative psychological impact. For school leavers who don't get accepted into university and then must go to the front, there is a double impact. One goes to the front not because you are a failure, but because it is a national duty, a national service. The current system actually diminishes the value of the front, which is a national duty for each citizen. We must have an ability to say to soldiers, and to all people, 'You may not be going to university now, but you'll be given other chances and other choices.'

"I don't, in fact, think that everybody in society can or should go to university," Mesgina concluded realistically. "There must be trade schools, and a variety of professions and skills must be taught. We don't have plumbers in this country, we need technicians, masons, and so forth."

In this regard, his perspective parallels that of Father Regazzo, and his pronouncements about the stages a society must go through seemed like the reasoned approach of a sage. As an elder statesman and an Eritrean who has worked deftly within the international arena, Mesgina holds views that are are respected if not always followed. His stewardship of a new project focusing on the country's culture is an example of how education, language, and culture are meant to mix — in the classic UNESCO sense.

Mesgina spoke with great excitement about the heritage project, officially known as the Cultural Assets Rehabilitation Project. With five basic programs — including site management and museums; building environments and historic areas; living cultures and oral tradition; archives and democratic accessibility;

and policy making and legislation — the hope of the project is to take some of the burdens off the MOE and other ministries and to guarantee that vital learning experiences be preserved for future generations. While in the historic Red Sea port city of Massawa, I was able to witness firsthand some of the extraordinary examples of architecture and design — some dating back centuries to periods of Egyptian and Turkish influence — intact but not well preserved. As I was told by the local head of the Ministry of Tourism, Yemawe Mekonnen, these are just the types of structures to be included in Mesgina's project, which was set to get off the ground late in 2001.

Mesgina, himself, retired and living in an apartment building in Asmara, was happy to remain a valued consultant, part of but not at the center of any official governmental position or office. "They asked me to become a member of the PFDJ [People's Front for Democracy and Justice], the political movement/party that evolved from the EPLF. I declined, not because I am not in agreement, but because there is no other party to join. Once I am given a choice and there are several parties to join, then I will choose to become part of the PFDJ!" Remaining concerned and open to friendly critiques regarding the direction of the country, Mesgina was basically hopeful about the future of Eritrea.

"Many of the government's policies are quite enlightened," he asserted. "They have been adopted to fit a multicultural, multilingual, and pluralist society. A fundamental principle for education, administration, and justice has been that every language is equal to all other languages, that every ethnic group has its own culture and should be proud of it. The government has given all the resources to these efforts, so that now the people will take on the stewardship of their own cultures. This is key for all of society, because to know your own culture is a link toward appreciating other cultures. And this, in turn, leads to tolerance.

"For us, the collection of oral histories in all of the languages of the country — using them in the schools, so that children know their parents' and grandparents' tales — is more than just a matter of education. The people must take care of their own heritages. Only in this way will they become masters of their own destinies."

* * *

The central office building of the People's Front for Democracy and Justice is awash in red, green, blue, and yellow, as flags, posters, and other paraphernalia mark ten years of transition. The PFDJ itself has officially replaced the EPLF, as a force leading political and economic matters in some respects parallel to the actual government ministries. A young and astute man heads the Ministry of Information from this building, hoping to open the way for greater participation and openness in education, journalism, and other public endeavors. My brief conversation with acting minister Zemhret Yohannes began with his assessment of education, in the past and today.

"Education has been basic to the whole process of liberation in Eritrea," he began, emphasizing a point that he has echoed through every interview. "It has always been stressed in all structures. In the military, it was particularly stressed, which is one of the reasons why we had an effective military process. Every unit of the army was encouraged to have its own cultural activities. And it was lively education — seen as an all-encompassing life experience, not for a specific space or time. What we're trying to do is to institutionalize this kind of outlook."[21]

Minister Yohannes, who currently serves as the Head of Research and Documentation and Executive Committee member of the PFDJ, described the process whereby every ministry within the government is designed to have an education-oriented department, where there is great care to remind government workers that Eritrea's fundamental resource is the human resource — one that cannot be neglected in the interests of natural resources or other concerns. "We can create material wealth," he noted, "but if it doesn't create a better life spiritually for the people where they can enjoy the riches and fruits of their own culture, then we will still have basic problems of development." He does not see secondary school education, despite all the issues and problems raised, as the main problem facing education. Agreeing that there is a long way to go as far as dealing with student-teacher ratios and the issue of opportunities open to school graduates, Yohannes emphatically stated that "we have to have the best teachers in elementary and junior education schools." It is there that the foundation is laid for a love of learning, culture, and country.

"I have a child in first grade and another in second grade," he shared, "and the fact that there are sixty students in a classroom is unacceptable! This is due to budgetary constraints, but it is what we are facing right now." He described the move to build more schools, making them as convenient as possible to each neighborhood and community. "Overall," he stated, "we don't have enough of a budget for what we want to do," which was another comment often repeated. He described, however, an initiative of summer work campaigns in education, where young people help with the building process, that is being used to supplement the work of the ministries. "We might not see huge progress in the short term, but in the long term, this creates values of solidarity, hard work, and community consciousness."

Careful to be neither overly negative nor overly optimistic, the minister spoke about the high quality of the 300 students attending university and the plans to increase that number to 1,000 by the end of 2002. Agreeing that one can't be excited about certain current practices like the problem of class size, he suggested that in a nation of thirty million, the number of high schools and technical schools (now roughly 40 and 6, respectively) needs to be at least doubled. "We'd like to stress what remains to be done," he concluded, with an undefeated sense of urgency. "We have to do it as soon as possible. If we don't have enough schools, we cannot move forward as a nation."[22]

Inside the national Ministry of Education building on the main street of downtown Asmara, securing an interview with the minister of education was not so easy a task. Originally a classroom teacher by trade, Osman Saleh Mohammed seemed now to be perpetually in meetings. On the first day back to work after the four-day independence weekend, he spent most of his time at the Office of the President. Stopping by his own office after official business hours were over, he allowed for some time to discuss general practices and future plans.

"Education for Eritrea has not been a matter of innovations," he said firmly, clearly tired but wanting to articulate in exact terms his views on the current state of affairs. "The EPLF as a movement, however, always made a priority of education for displaced persons, for the children of martyrs, the children of fighters, and so forth. The more we liberated various parts of the country, the more we expanded education for a wide variety of children. In 1983, we went behind enemy lines, conducting the literacy programs. Always, we've worked under the principle that emancipation of the people could only happen through knowledge."[23]

"After liberation, with an entire country to serve, the supply could simply not meet up with the demand. With geographic disparities, and gender disparities as well, we had a plan for equal-opportunity education for all Eritreans, but implementation was confined to a very small area. We still believe that the issue of gender inequality can be solved only through education and are trying to work in a very united form, respecting people's culture and diversity. We have tried our utmost for our people to have full educational access, but this is still a big issue for us."

Minister Osman related, confirming the reports of others, that the need to train more teachers was a high priority. He noted that teaching materials for grades one through five have been prepared in eight languages and are now being completed for the ninth. The plans for junior and high school education, to take place in English, Arabic, and Tigrinya, were still under way, but people's displacement during the three-year war affected some of those plans. Nevertheless, literacy from the time of independence had gone from 160,000 people in 1991 to 442,000 by May 2001. Mother tongue had been encouraged through capacity-building development. Still, the minister suggested, "the government is facing a really big challenge." Education is inextricably linked, he asserted, to the very preservation of culture.

"I wish and I believe that all ethnic groups will participate in all walks of life — economic, political, social, and cultural," Osman concluded, with a sense of passion coming through the fatigue of a long day. "If this takes place, then it means that the unity of Eritrea has been achieved. This, we know, can only take place through education. That is why the government is working very hard to bring education to all people and to make it relevant to their lives."

Whether the words of Ministers Zemhret or Osman helped enhance one's understanding of the problems of modern-day Eritrean educational practice depends largely on one's own political orientation and expectations. Politicians, whatever their commitments to liberation or to "the people," are never in a position to tell a story fully, least of all to an outsider, speaking on the record for a relatively short period of time. Even so, listening closely to their carefully chosen words, a pattern can be seen to emerge. There is a consistency regarding the nature of the current challenges. That these are spoken of openly, from the grassroots level of teachers and learners to the halls of the decision-makers, is at least a positive step. Though there are fairly wide variances in the degrees of optimism or pessimism about future possibilities, there is one other key point of agreement: whatever the magnitude of the crisis today, the gains since independence have been both visible and significant. This, in a ten-year period, is no small matter.

* * *

The space for discussion in contemporary Eritrean civil society — among nongovernmental organizations (NGOs), the educated elite, and the majority of the population outside of the urban centers — had just begun to develop and grow at the time of the tenth anniversary. Some groups, like the Asmara-based Citizens for Peace (CPE), had focused much of their energy on strategically narrow popular education campaigns — as in CPE's work documenting the uprooted refugees deported by Ethiopia during the three-year war. Still, the country's determination about the profits of unity in diversity permeated these discussions in often interesting ways. CPE leader Professor Asmarom Legesse, a Harvard-trained scholar and author of numerous works on indigenous African identity in the Horn of Africa, made a special effort to reach out to NGOs in Ethiopia and other parts of the region. "We have to be able to reach out across years of war and division," he noted during a private conversation, "to find out what we can learn that is rich and good about each other's cultures and traditions."[24]

Far and away the most powerful NGO, linked closely to the government but officially independent, is the National Union of Eritrean Youth and Students (NUEYS). With over 135,000 members in all towns, villages, and schools, NUEYS carries out an educational agenda all its own. Most notably, it has been and continues to be partly responsible for the push for gender equity and has both supported governmental education efforts and run its own campaigns, with posters, T-shirts, and meetings discussing the importance of educating female youth. When I asked NUEYS's national chairperson, Mohiadin Shengeb, to talk about NUEYS's work in light of the general educational problems facing the country, his first response was modest: "Ten years is quite a short time to evaluate the result of planning for all the dreams we have had for Eritrea."

"We have done a lot," Shengeb continued, "but we are far from being able to say that we have created a change in terms of thinking. We have seen dramatic growth in the field of education, as far as the increased numbers of people going to school, the benefits and standards of students. But the difficult part is when it comes to changes in attitude — how education is really a means of changing people's lifestyles, economic conditions, et cetera. This has been especially true regarding the role of girls in society. But this is not a short-term issue that you can make change quickly."

In describing the work of NUEYS, Shengeb noted that "when you talk of education, you can't help talking about politics" — a refrain popular in Frierean pedagogy. In attempting to confront an anticipated problem regarding post-high school unemployment over the first years of the new millennium, NUEYS has entered into the political discussions about technical versus university education, with a perspective that suggests that youth be trained to go back to work in their original "home" communities. There are six major project areas that the organization is concerned with, working in each of these with a democratic, bottom-to-top decision-making structure. In addition to its work in education, NUEYS has projects relating to health (especially regarding HIV/AIDS peer counseling and condom distribution), employment, gender equity (a subset of several projects as well as a project in and of itself), the environment, leisure and sports activities, and popular participation.

"Our work in the field of education," Shengeb told me, "has been to participate as volunteers in the literacy campaigns, to encourage girls especially, and to set up contests, prizes, and nonformal tactics to get people involved. For vocational support after graduation, we've been reaching agreements with people in the private sector — to set up workshops to provide training and possible job placement. From these trainings, young people can decide what kind of work they truly want to do — and often these technical trades, and not the office jobs, are the best-paid jobs in the country.

"We also promote 'informal' education through the publication of student newspapers, drama, music, the fine arts, and dialogues with families. In some of these cases, NUEYS would start a project that the MOE or Ministry of Information would eventually take up as one of their own. In the area of participation, we are targeting young people to get involved in politics....We now have a big project specifically looking at the Constitution's position on elections, translating materials into all the different languages so that all people will be able to participate. Though there have been no national governmental elections yet, the government says that it is good that we have been conducting these campaigns."

Listening to the list of NUEYS activities and getting a sampling of their posters and propaganda, one feels that a special process is taking place here. Though now looking to break up into smaller, more manageable suborganizations, NUEYS is, by percentage at least, the largest youth organization on the continent and one of the largest in the world. Developing a five-year plan and navigating carefully in a postwar period full of potential transitions and much open critique of Eritrea's top officials, NUEYS is still a vibrant and unapologetic champion of the Eritrean ideals of multilingualism, consensus-building, and equality. At a time in Eritrea of growing questions, on a continent with continuing problems, this grassroots organization is a vibrant source of hope.

* * *

The uncomfortable truth is that education in Eritrea, on the whole, has not lived up to the promises or the policies laid out in the EPLF's original dreams or the actual efforts of the pre-independence campaigns. Minister Osman Saleh Mohammed may have hit on the most important point, though indirectly: The liberation movement was simply unprepared for the demands of educating an entire country, not simply a mobilized liberated zone or area under attack. Social-change activists and educators should well appreciate that fighting a common enemy is almost always easier than forging a positive program. It is also true that, throughout history and across borders, those working for liberation have just barely begun to review the possibilities, meaning, and problematics of "winning" a given struggle. Eritrea is not exempt from these global dynamics, though one might have hoped that four decades of war would have created some greater space for planning, and members of the educated Eritrean community at home and abroad might now wish for such an exemption.

Indeed, in the years since the tenth anniversary, troubling indications that Eritrea's national leadership has grown less tolerant of dissent and more open to reactionary multinational influences have permeated reports from the country. One correspondent asserted that "education is dead," referring to rumors rampant throughout 2003 that secondary school education would no longer be free. Disturbing reports suggested that Eritrea was adopting a controversial "Essential Knowledge and Skills" standardized assessment tool developed in Texas, with barely a modification to fit the complex Eritrean cultural context. Eritrean leader at the Constitutional Commission Paulos Tesfagiorgis, awarded the prestigious European Rafto Prize for human rights in 2003, has stated that the 1998 war with Ethiopia changed everything for Eritrea's progressive policies.

"Every aspect of national life," he stated in 2004 from exile in the U.S.A., "has become subordinate to the security and military exigency of the country."[25] Nevertheless, often-critical sources such as the United Nations Development Programme — not one to sugarcoat their analysis of troubled areas — wrote of contemporary Eritrean struggles in light of the economic, political, and emotional turmoil of the border war. Eritrea is shifting, they suggested, from a "relief to a recovery" mode.[26]

The phrase "Victory to the Masses" — for Eritrea and for the world — must be an ongoing mantra. The masses, common folk in the countryside, have definitely benefited the most from Eritrea's independence movement; calls for victory in the future must be more than hollow slogans. Nor should such calls of victory be used as triumphant batons, to wave above the heads of doubters or dissenters. Victory in Eritrea was not achieved in 1991 or 1993 and certainly not at the end of the three-year war. Working for massive transformation, as this short look at educational practices shows, cannot be completed in a single "moment" of final fulfillment. Even in a revolutionary setting such as a movement for national liberation, the struggles for the transformation of people's ways of thinking, as Shengeb put it, take generations at least. Whether the ideals of Eritrea's educational planners come closer to fruition in five years or ten is a matter of speculation and future struggle. Now, one can only definitively state that, despite and in light of the many disappointments, much can still be learned from reviewing the educational process of this newest of African nations.

Chapter 8

WORKING WITHIN THE U.S. PRESSURE COOKER

> [We] must try to avoid the mistakes that some countries, such as the U.S., have made, where painful experiences resulting from colonization, slavery and racism are not discussed openly, in the classroom or elsewhere. These issues are not discussed because "they are too painful to talk about," and are "things of the past," and society must not dwell on things of the past.
>
> — Maqhudeni Ivy Goduka
> *Affirming Unity in Diversity in Education*

Learning from our South African colleagues, it seems wrongheaded to begin a critique or analysis of U.S. alternative education without connecting first with our own voices, our own identities, discussing things not usually considered in educational manuals or conventional comparative studies.

My own personal narrative could start off with these basics: my physical apparatus suggests male gender, a suggestion I have always felt comfortable with, though some of my more challenging profeminist friends insist that "refusing to be a man" is on the agenda of any truly antisexist, antipatriarchal program.[1] My skin tone and assumed racial status in society is that of a white person, although I'm especially appreciative of my Native American colleagues who have pointed out that the word "white" has always connoted a purity, and white folks in U.S. and African societies have acted far from innocently. I prefer to call and think of myself as "of European descent," which is a literal fact. That both my parents and two of my grandparents were born in Brooklyn doesn't diminish the fact that my father's mother and most of my mother's mother's family came to the U.S. through Ellis Island and the Jewish migrations from Austria-Hungary and Poland of the late nineteenth/early twentieth century. Culturally, I am Jewish. My two grandmothers were raised in Orthodox homes, but practiced mainly in the Conservative branch of the religion. One old friend insightfully (incitefully?) calls our generation one of "devout Jewish atheists"[2] — and that seems to fit, though I have my more spiritual moments when I meld my partner's parents' religions (one branch Quaker, one branch Protestant) with my own, to make an interesting Judeo-Christian mish-mosh. Like many of my generation, I am aware that previous generations of our "chosen people" in Europe were not considered white, but that in U.S. society we certainly are. I live out this privilege by trying to celebrate as many diverse religious holidays as is possible. Though I use the word "partner" to describe my primary relationship with my mutually monogamous soulmate, and we struggle politically and practically to live out what would be considered by many a queer existence, there can be no denying the fact that my partner is a woman. Some years ago, we bought a brownstone in Brooklyn, with some financial help from our parents. Though the bank still owns all but one faucet of one sink of one bathroom, that still makes me out to be a straight, white, property-owning male.

My personal narrative *could* start out that way, and it does get certain demographics out of the way, but I'd prefer to start it like this: "America has never been a melting pot. America today, as it has been for decades, is much more like a pressure cooker. And the pressure is building up...."

What these words, which I believe to be true, have to do with Matt Meyer's personal narrative is that I wrote them as a junior in high school — a clever turn of phrase that got me some recognition at the time, though I had little understanding of what they truly meant in a historical or on an intergroup basis. Those words are important not simply because they are still relevant, but because there is no doubt that my enjoyment of, cleverness in, and recognition during my years at Brooklyn's experimental

Edward R. Murrow High School played a significant role in my becoming a high school teacher and teacher-trainer later in life.

In fact, my connection to the world of New York City public high schools goes back to 1968, the infamous Ocean-hill-Brownsville strike, and a small vocational-technical school in the Brighton Beach section of Brooklyn. My memories are fairly strong, though I was quite young, of a very disturbed father — United Federation of Teachers chapter leader at William E. Grady High School — coming home distraught, worried, confused, and/or angry. Simon Meyer remained a faithful chapter chair for many years, through shifting political winds, until the rights of teachers were well entrenched within the city Board of Education bureaucracy. More importantly, to him and to me, he remained a faithful servant of his students for over thirty years, teaching English with a passion and a flair unmatched by most of his other endeavors. He poured out Shakespeare to his kids, but in 1969 he also took in the then-recent Beatles album *Sergeant Pepper's Lonely Hearts Club Band*, having his kids dissect the poem "A Day in the Life." My folks were not hippies, radicals, or protesters; the UFT work for my dad and some community-based charitable fund-raising for my mom were as close as they came to activism. Simon's own reflections on the 1968 strike changed over time, as I became a college activist years later — first decrying, then personally befriending the complex figure that was Bayard Rustin. I had only a fleeting understanding of those messy times.[3]

The other formative part of my childhood was molded most concretely by my two feisty grandmothers, who knew each other all their lives and lived in the same apartment building off Kings Highway since before I was born. Their fiercely competitive, intensely loving counter-dynamics made an indelible mark. Sylvia's stories of fleeing Poland one step ahead of the Tsarist army, watching her town being burned to the ground moments after her brothers, mother, and she had fled, and Mollie's common-sense teachings ("character above all") each helped send me on my own political trajectory. They lived most of their adult lives without men, helping each other and building their families. My mother, Marilyn, mixed their tenacity with a certain softer pragmatism and humor that has stayed within me to this day. Economically, my grandparents were working class, barely surviving, and my parents strove toward a middle-class lifestyle, only without the money to pay the bills. That was the part of the pressure cooker I felt growing up and why demographics only partly do justice to narratives.

* * *

Somewhere along the line, like the sons of many a high school English teacher (Mick Jagger comes quickly to mind), I definitively decided that I would not, under any circumstances, follow in my father's footsteps. The field of law seemed promising; pursuing acting or the professional music industry seemed far too risky, and when I began to become centrally involved in the U.S. peace movements of the early 1980s,[4] becoming a historian of contemporary social movements appeared more and more attractive. The consistently covert and occasionally overt institutional racism of the antinuclear and antidraft coalitions I was a part of (pointed out, most notably, by Black veterans organizations and individuals and by Pan-African organizations under the leadership of Kwame Ture/Stokely Carmichael), led me directly into a desire to study revolutions of the so-called Third World; my African and Latin American undergraduate history degree left me wanting greater information and contact. Bills had to be paid, however, and the seesaw nature of the Board of Education's policy of hiring too many teachers with low pay and few rights one year and facing massive "layoffs,"[5] teacher retirements, or a general teacher shortage the next was swinging in the direction of hiring. With no education credits to my name, and my "Mick Jagger decision" and fascination with African studies firmly in my mind, I signed up, agreeing to take twelve education credits within four semesters, telling the placement center that I'd work anywhere they'd send me, and promising myself that I'd be out of the system before the end of three years.

Sterling High School, where I was sent to teach math (a field I was clearly qualified in, having taken the bare requirement of one three-credit math course my freshman year in college), was an all-boys school in Brooklyn's Fort Greene neighborhood. Sterling was where young men were sent who had been described by the school system as "severely emotionally handicapped." In fact, with an almost nonexistent psychological or social work staff, Sterling contained their students, whose main handicap was extreme and volatile anger at their circumstances, with sometimes extreme discipline and always tight structure. The structure, I believe, was in many ways liberating, and when the bell rang and students came into a class facing a teacher who showed that he or she really wanted to impart some knowledge and partake in some dialogue, learning took place. At some moments, such as when a few of us created the school's first literary magazine, the structure and mutual respect and information-sharing between students and staff shifted for a moment away from the chaos and pressure cooker of their lives to create safe, teachable spaces.

It was no coincidence that, in all of New York City, there were no white public high school students labeled "severely emotionally handicapped." Two African American deans served as the school father figures, and one distinguished gentleman, seen and treated as a community elder, ran a barber shop that truly transmitted practical, vocational skills to the boys who were ready to "settle down." The rest of the school leadership — administration, union reps, department heads, and clinicians — were all white, with a few young and talented Black teachers (and me) at the bottom of the totem pole, causing trouble. The majority of the young men enrolled at Sterling were too disgusted at or disconnected from the melting pot mythology that had never included them to buy into the education that some of us were trying to provide. Extremely street-smart and savvy about interpersonal dynamics, they could detect a sniffle from a thirty-yard distance and knew if a teacher came in sick, unprepared, or simply too tired to give them the attention they craved and deserved. To preempt what must have been their nineteen hundredth disappointment, they caused havoc in the classroom before an unsuspecting teacher could cause boredom.

In my first several months, at least two major disruptions occurred in my room, with chairs literally flung across the room and tables turned upside down. After fourteen-plus years in the business, and many fine high school graduates and college students now having passed through my doors whose names I've long forgotten, I still clearly remember the faces and names of some of those guys whose buttons I pushed, after they had pushed mine. Eric, a foot taller than I and often drugged out by the time he came to class in the morning, was in training to become a ninja. One day he decided to throw a sharply studded, six-cornered Asian karate star at my head, missing me by several feet but becoming wedged firmly in the blackboard behind me. Not missing a beat, I unwedged the star, placed it in my pocket, and continued the lesson as best I could until the bell rang. At the end of the period, Eric asked for his weapon back, amazed that I would consider denying him his property. He walked me angrily and anxiously to the dean's office, apparently unaware that the issue of brandishing a weapon in school might be taken more seriously by the dean than that of his property loss! I left the two of them to debate the issue, ninja star and all.

At the end of each day at Sterling, I spent one hour on the IRT train lines, heading north to Columbia University Teachers College (TC). In addition to getting the required twelve credits and a license in the teaching of social studies, I spent most of my time in Columbia's other graduate departments, taking any advanced-study courses on Africa I could find. These I linked into a TC program inhabited mainly by teachers studying from abroad, in a specialized master's program on International Education Development (IED). Heavily influenced by the Department of Comparative Education, for which TC was renowned, the IED program enabled me to complete a thesis on postindependence educational systems in Mozambique and Zimbabwe. My first trip to Africa, working briefly in those two countries to assemble information and begin a lifelong process of networking, took place in this context. The world turned upside down for me, as the shining spirit of the women of Maputo seared in my heart while the fate of the boys of Fort Greene weighed on my soul.

Columbia University, at this time, was experiencing some turmoil that my generation was not supposed to be known for. Hamilton Hall was shut down by a long-lasting student strike, calling for university divestment from the banks of apartheid South Africa. Activism followed graduate and doctoral students, despite our supposed desires to focus on study. Some demands were ultimately met, but not before campuses throughout the country erupted with similar student involvement. After an intense eighteen months of seesawing between the two worlds of Sterling and Columbia, with anti-apartheid activism fitting in between the edges, I took a brief, unpaid leave of absence. Though I conscientiously arranged for a friend to take over my classes at Sterling while I was gone,[6] I was shocked to learn that by the time the school year was over, my position at the high school nobody wanted to teach at had somehow evaporated. My Columbia degree, however, was also finished, and I attended the ceremonies — complete with a student walkout to protest Columbia's racist attitudes toward the Harlem community[7] — not quite knowing my next career steps.

Being "excessed" from one school to another — perhaps one of the most humiliating experiences in our "professional" pantheon of errors — I was finally appointed to the huge downtown Manhattan high school my grandmother had once attended: Washington Irving. At the time, it was trying to remodel itself as Washington Irving High School of International Studies and Foreign Languages, so it appeared that creating a niche might be possible. Throughout this time, while I expected at any moment to find a suitable non-Board of Education African studies position, I was mentored by various teacher-trainers who suggested that, once you close your classroom door, magic could take place.[8]

One year, I experienced the all-too-common mistake of being asked to assist an assistant principal. The idea that good teachers should be "logically" promoted into administrative positions has robbed many classrooms of people whose real competencies lie there. Though organizationally minded, I found the bureaucracy mind-numbing and raced back to a full-time teaching load for what was to be a critical following year. I was so glad to be out of the office (and, though remaining friendly, the administrators were happy to see me go!). I put special emphasis on my day-to-day technique, focusing much attention on Africa and Latin America for a freshman global studies course. At the end of that June, my sixth full year teaching, I began to think that it might be possible to merge my passions for African studies, social change, and high school education.

The boys at Sterling, though, are the real heroes of this story. Many of them were strikingly creative, with flashes of brilliance in their poetry and art. Most were simply striking out at each other, going through a revolving door of bad schools, prisons, and a street life that ensured only the most short-term survival. They were perfect examples of what Paulo Freire meant when he said, talking to a U.S. interviewer, "Maybe so many people emerge from your school systems illiterate because they are resisting, refusing to read the world the way they're being taught it."[9] For the Sterling boys, their resistance required a refusal not only of the school system itself, but of the society as well.

They did not give respect unless they got it. They could not pay attention unless they were convinced that it would be rewarded by relevant and useful information. And they would never include educators in their internal dialogues unless they were sure that those educators would fight for them before fighting for any system or self-interest that had long since sold them out. Through all of their actions and reactions, they taught me, more surely than anyone else, how to become a transformative teacher.

* * *

The lines between personal narrative and professional development treatise began to blur as I entered New York's alternative high schools in 1989. Supported from the outset in ways I had barely imagined possible working within the city's special-education or industrial factory-school settings, I was given the space to explore all of my passions simultaneously: a space rarely found in any job setting. Though far from perfect, the alternative superintendency allowed for teacher creativity, supported the ideas of student-centered learning, and encouraged collaboration between staff at all levels and our local communities. Extraordinarily diverse in its makeup alone — including schools located in the prisons of Riker's Island, programs working in partnership with the U.S. Department of Labor, and a school-without-walls based on internship programs — the superintendency always attracted both the above-average, super-creative teenagers and the "at-risk" ones. The district has always had a multiethnic, multilingual orientation. Several of our schools were specifically designed for dual Chinese-English and Spanish-English instruction, so that new immigrants could excel in their current environment, in part by maintaining a strong basis in their mother tongue.

This is not to say that all educators mainly need to expand and join the alternative schools movement. Many young teachers were consistently attracted by rumors or information similar to the above promotional-sounding message, only to be severely turned off by the fact that bureaucracy within the superintendency *did* exist; administrators could be blindsided by institutional racism, sexism, ageism, homophobia. The pressures of the Central Board of Education and mainstream society played major roles in affecting the alternative schools. Some of us often felt that the alternative superintendency was a bad place to begin one's career in education. Without understanding the structures and the struggles of the regular school system, inexperienced educators were often caught tightly between the apparent contradiction of their personal visions (often positive) and a school's own day-to-day realities (often fraught with fiscal and other limitations). By the time I became part of what came to be titled New York's "alternative, adult, and continuing education schools and programs," I had already earned a second postgraduate degree in educational psychology and was fully embroiled in an "after-school" project, collaborating with Bill Sutherland to produce what would become the book *Guns and Gandhi in Africa: Pan-Africanist Insights on Nonviolence, Armed Struggle and Liberation* (2000). My years as an organizer had honed in me a sense of the strategic; approaching politics within the alternative superintendency would be a matter of carefully working within the confines of "the possible" — pushing those boundaries when- and wherever appropriate.

Within two years, at a time when "education that is multicultural" was made a priority by the chancellor and the Central Board, several of us from different schools set up a citywide multicultural committee, and in 1993 I became its coordinator — a position I served in until 2002. During those years of service, four broad areas of concern surfaced in my mind, which subsequently seem most significant in building transformative schools. These areas reflect the roots of the various professional development and curricular enhancement projects New York City's alternative educators have worked on these past years — the best of what we were hoping to achieve. These four foundations — (1) working under the leadership of oppressed communities, especially the Black and Puerto Rican progressive movements; (2) working in a practical way that would ensure accessibility and relevance to a diversity of students and staff; (3) working within the context of a peace philosophy of coalition-building and networking; and (4) working to link with colleagues across district, national, and international lines — were reached in an uneven manner at best. But they speak to an attempt to build a base for empowering education that has proven all but impossible in most parts of the United States.

ROOTED IN THE STRUGGLES OF THE BLACK AND LATINA COMMUNITIES

One cannot truly understand the nature of education and social change without dealing with a given community's fight for self-determination and power. Within this context, one must also comprehend the dialectical relationship between reformist and radical models for change and how they often complement (or are co-opted) by one another. There are few cases more clear or significant in this regard than that of the Black Panther Party for Self-Defense (BPP). While the BPP is remembered historically for its gun-toting members and its uncompromising rhetoric against "pigs," its uncompromising commitment to the needs of its community led Panthers to set up a breakfast program for children, years before comprehensive, all-day school food and nutrition programs were introduced.[10] When former Panther leader Jamal Joseph spoke to a New York City alternative schools conference of students and staff, he reinforced the ideals of serving the community. However, now he was using drama and the arts as his weapon, working as artistic director of City Kids and his own Harlem-based program.[11] Long after the destruction of the BPP, due largely to the government's illegal counterintelligence program (COINTELPRO), school systems across the country have taken up the need to provide a cross-section of the population with basic dietary needs before providing basic educational needs. The reality may be corn chips and old textbooks, but the dream is bread and roses, too.

Another organization born of the 1960s civil rights and Black liberation movements but with important connections to educational transformation today is SNCC, the Student Nonviolent (later "National") Coordinating Committee. In addition to emphasizing a grassroots organizing approach that made a priority of working with entire families, working within the context of a given community's realities, and placing a special significance on the power of youth, SNCC produced some extraordinary leaders who continue to influence teaching today. Stokely Carmichael/Kwame Ture, perhaps the best known and most controversial, is remembered for his fiery proclamations for Black Power, suggesting "Hell, no," Black youth wouldn't fight in the white man's war in Vietnam. Ture was, in fact, one of the most fiercely committed advocates for students and youth up till the very end of his life. Choosing to build organizations rather than schools, Ture traveled tirelessly around the globe speaking at conferences and on campuses to large and small groupings of young people.[12] In one of his last formal interviews, the conversation he granted to alternative schools student leaders, he advised that, in addition to getting a complete and critical education, they needed to "organize, organize, organize."[13]

At the other end of the SNCC political spectrum, soft-spoken Bob Moses has taken the lessons of the Southern-based "freedom now" movement to his contemporary campaigns for math literacy. Using an experiential, inquiry-based approach, Moses's

Algebra Project is founded on the premise that the changing nature of global economics necessitates a knowledge of higher math skills if one is to acquire true liberation. Having spent time teaching in Tanzania, Moses has incorporated his experiences there by including a curricular unit on African drums to teach about ratios, rates, and fractions. He has emphasized the power of students' imaginations over the memorization and drill techniques so common in traditional math courses. In accepting a peace award from a New York-based national pacifist organization, Moses made the connections between civil rights, Pan-Africanism, and educational change. In her introduction of Moses, alternative high schools deputy superintendent Margaret Bing-Wade, then president of the National Alliance of Black School Educators, spoke of the importance of his contributions, however indirect, to our communities and our schools.[14]

Another, less prominent African American activist-educator personifies an entirely different but related tradition of community service. Mimsie Robinson, a deacon of his Harlem-based "born again" Christian church, may not be the most obvious candidate among leaders of radical social change. There can be no doubt, however, of the significance of the role of the organized Black church in grounding the movements of the past decades. This fact, one often overlooked by northerners, city dwellers, and progressives with an overly simplistic view of the "separation" or "collusion" between church and state, is nonetheless indispensable in understanding the nature of positive community-building common to almost all "oppressed nationalities."

The roots of Robinson's "agenda" may be fundamentally different than the agendas of the "average" leftist (if such a thing ever did or still exists), but for the purpose of examining transformative techniques, the effects of his personalized, student-centered methodology are little different than those of the methods used by the other activists cited here. Robinson's early work was as the math and science educator in a one-room, two-teacher East Harlem alternative site set up in the corner of a Human Resources Administration (HRA) building.[15] HRA had been involved in a recent lawsuit that required them to provide some hours of learning to homeless kids who were awaiting permanent residential placement. They came in with a bag full of all their worldly belongings, not knowing where they'd spend that night or whether they'd be back to the "Teen Lounge" the next day. No credit could be given for the hours or days they spent in this setting, so there was little incentive to work. Some students were functionally illiterate, others quite bright, and all in deep trauma — mostly not of their own making. The seriousness, loving-kindness, flexibility, and creativity of Robinson's approach cut through the devastating moments to connect with most of these youngsters. There was no cursing in this classroom, but plenty of space for the expression of one's needs and feelings. Though HRA closed the lounge after some months, Robinson took these same skills and methods to work as senior guidance counselor at the more academically oriented Unity High School within the alternative schools. In 1997, he was recognized as New York State Teacher of the Year.

The challenge for liberatory educators, to stay rooted within community-based struggles and movements led by peoples working to break free from a history of subjugation, may seem easier than it is. It requires an analysis of power dynamics within society that places these struggles at the center of any real or lasting social transformation. It also requires an understanding of why the power dynamic between teacher and student is so significant: not because teachers need to be weakened, but because a new world will only spring forth from the ideas of future generations. The challenges of globalization and the lessons of those advocating technical colleges in Eritrea spring to mind when reviewing this summary by Bob Moses:

"The key," he writes in *Radical Equations: Math Literacy and Civil Rights* (Moses and Cobb, 2001), "is that the young people have to figure out how to organize themselves. Math literacy, like voter registration, provides them with a tool for such work.... [They have to] figure out how they can use this intellectual capital to really generate income and resources necessary for survival over the long haul. This is the issue of the change in technology from technology around physical work to a technology around mental thought, where a lot of the capital is intellectual capital. They have to understand that part of their function is to marshal their intellectual capital and put it to work for themselves if they are to avoid getting in a situation where they are just posturing, believing that what is important is holding office, or just being in an office, as opposed to really doing work.... [They've] got the problem of convincing other people — whether in voter registration or in education — that the idea of challenging yourself and the system that defines your life is an idea to be embraced."[16]

ROOTED IN A PRACTICE ACCESSIBLE AND RELEVANT TO YOUNG PEOPLE AND TO ALL STAFF

"Empowerment" may be the word of the moment among some progressive teacher-trainers; "student-centered" was last year's phrase. The root meanings of a "liberatory" or even "transformative" education, used often in this text, may not be apparently clear or universally understood. "Liberated from what?" one may ask; "transformed" into what? Beyond the simpler suggestions that liberation and transformation need take place from a racist, sexist, homophobic, economistic society to one of equity, equality, justice, and peace lie the "how-to" questions about getting from here to there. In addition, ageism — an oppression all of us have experienced, some of us have successfully "grown out of," and some of us may encounter again if we live long enough — is nevertheless part of a damning series of social dynamics that suggest that authoritarian power over one group of people is acceptable. This is not an internationally endorsed idea, it should be noted, as some cultures honor their elders and others suggest that young people need actually take the lead — as "medicine for one's soul" or windows to a world of wonder.[17]

In designing curriculum, programs, or institutions for students and all staff, one focus must center around accessibility and relevance. Those tough boys at Sterling or traumatized teens at HRA knew immediately when something presented to them was being delivered "over their heads" or outside of the scope of what would be useful to them. While lacking many skills to survive in mainstream society, they felt the power to speak up and demand that something be changed. It is no coincidence that gifted and talented youngsters more often than not display similar characteristics; if the teachings are not "on point," they will become fidgety, disruptive, and often vocal about the need for new material. Unhappily, the vast majority of more docile students, who, by the time they get to high school, have already had some expectations of the wonders and magic of learning something new and useful long since dashed or beaten out of them (sometimes literally), remain quiet.

This is not to say for a moment that the job of schools or teacher-trainers is to design frameworks that will always make children happy, to spoon-feed at all times that which is familiar and considered fun. But being interesting, engaging, respectful, conscientious, challenging, and stimulating is at the core of any good education. Educational psychologist Lev Vygotsky wrote of the need to speak "just above the heads" of potential learners[18] — not in a paternalistic way but to facilitate both high expectations and a dynamic dialogue of information transference. Simply being mindful of some of these dynamics and the realities of ageism faced by all of our "subjects" — staying aware of the great power we have as teachers, even though we often feel powerless in the shadow of a huge bureaucracy — is a humble start. Using that power positively, to listen to our students, have them learn from one another, and share some of the magic of life we've picked up and retained along the way, is ultimately our job.

Within the alternative superintendency, the Professional Development, Multicultural Advisory, and other committees struggled to set an example in these areas through a number of different techniques and projects. First by networking and discussing these issues among our diverse student and staff populations, then by creating curriculum that would help bridge the gaps, our own practice was full of mainly community and local school-based successes. We valued student authorship and published countless booklets and books of student writings, including an incredible initiative on student literacy from within the prison schools on Riker's Island.[19] This effort was led by then-principal Tim Lisante, who went on to become Superintendent of Alternative High Schools (2005-2006) only to be undermined and ultimately removed because of his strong student advocacy. We developed student leadership courses, teaching basic organizing, public speaking, conflict resolution, and peer education skills, giving the students the resources and space to shape their own annual conferences on issues chosen, researched, and presented by them.[20] In conjunction with the Central Board Office on Multicultural Education, we set up countless seminars for staff, including a graduate-level, three-credit professional development course, where all these issues were dealt with in greater depth. Mini-libraries of some of the most exciting new literature on all of these topics and in every subject area were distributed to each of our schools every year, in the hopes that these innovative resources would be shared among the appropriate pedagogues and participants. And a book of our own, *Multicultural Voices in Action*, was published in 1995 that served as a compendium of best practices taking place within our schools.

Networking and sharing new ideas — helping staff as well as students feel their power and exercise it positively — was a hallmark of our practice. Annual conferences were organized to bring students and staff together, with a variety of featured speakers designed to capture the imaginations of both groups simultaneously. Presenters over the years have included deputy chancellors, directors of instruction and Board of Education member Esmerelda Simmons. Popular cultural figures, such as hip-hop icons Sister Souljah and Talib Kweli of Black Star and poets Lindamichellebaron and asha bandele, have donated their time and services. Authors Walter Dean Meyers, Beverly Singer, David Lamb, and numerous others have encouraged students to write their own stories and connect with their own voices. In 1990, at one of our first major events, American Indian leader and cofounder of the Indigenous Women's Network, Ingrid Washinawatok, took the stage, passionately describing her own upbringing and urging her audience to take charge of their own lives.[21]

At one plenary, noted educator, sociologist, children's book author, and lawyer, Dr. Luis Nieves Falcon of the University of Puerto Rico, helped sharpen the definitions of our most often-used terms. Going beyond simply broadening access or increasing interest, he challenged educators and students alike to understand "relevance" as a concept that reexamines our histories and current realities. Coming from a circumstance of direct U.S. colonialism, and having just worked as a consultant for the Chicago Board of Education in conjunction with a nationally award-winning private high school in the heart of that city's Puerto Rican community,[22] Dr. Nieves Falcon described the process of change in his own work:

"We started off from various principles," he began, "among them that education is a reflection of the dominant forces in a particular society. As such, education is an important structure of the state, and as such, one of its principal goals is to assure acceptance of the existing order and to internalize prevailing hierarchical laws of governance." On the other hand, "education that is multicultural educates the students to become analytical thinkers, capable of examining their personal situations, including a class-based clarification that keeps them from reaping social benefits and economic rewards to assure their full development. In a sense, in this concern, our multicultural strategy is conceived as a liberation strategy....In a sense, [a] school's entire concept [has] to change, in that it [must begin] to see itself not only as a school for students, as a school for the school-aged population, but as a transformed instrument for the self-realization of the students, the parents, and the whole community."[23]

In this instance, the school must be brought into the community, and the community must become engaged in the education of the student. New York's alternative high schools, for all our good works and attempts, still struggle to reach these ambitions and essential goals. We must reflect upon how the work of a given project or the energy of a particular conference can be dispersed to reach not just the already committed, but the majority of teachers in the majority of our schools, incorporating this work and this energy into the majority of day-to-day practice. In this sense, our own struggles to create transformed spaces within the schools of the urban United States reflect, in very real ways, a similar set of issues faced by progressive educators of emerging nations throughout the world.

Once achieved, as Dr. Nieves Falcon reminded us, "new, participatory roles for students [will be] identified, in which students become active participants in decisions affecting their own lives — like school discipline and socio-cultural enrichment." It will take no less than a "restructuring of the whole information base" in order to "make visible the invisible, to make equal the unequal, to make worthy the unworthy."[24]

ROOTED IN A PEACE PHILOSOPHY OF COALITION-BUILDING

Strategic and tactical alliances, building bridges across political and ideological lines, are appropriate and necessary in the field of education no less than in any significant organizing arena. Though the coalitions may be made up of sectors and individuals more than between well-established organizations and the ideologies may be less clear or overt than among partisan political groups, principled decisions must be made at all times. School-based coalition-building must discern who may be worked with, who *must* be included, and who should be approached with care or confrontation. Novices may confuse principles with political correctness, but we've found little use for holier-than-thou attitudes in managing successful cross-professional efforts.

One ironic example of how this has manifested itself in the multicultural field is the various practical interpretations of James Banks's four levels of the "multicultural ladder": the heroes and holidays approach, the additive approach, the transformative approach, and the social change model. In an attempt at multicultural correctness and sophistication, overzealous organizers will often skip over a meaningful step and alienate an entire sector of the school or local community. Sometimes food festivals *really are* important events for bringing people together, so long as there is no pretending that we've all always had an equal place at the dinner table or an equal share of the pie. Struggling to push an institution (like a department or an entire school) to take part in social change activities is a lofty ideal, but as we have seen in a myriad of South African examples, ideals do not always translate into good practice. Our principles should suggest that we are always trying to work effectively in moving together up the ladder toward lasting change. This is a long process and never a single, accepted motion, as in, "Okay, we're now a social change school." Even though one of New York's alternative sites was called the Coalition School for Social Change, engaged in some excellent work in many progressive fields, and another of our more successful schools is connected to the progressive trade union 1199 (health and hospital workers), it is still necessary to remember that radical change and a transformed institutional orientation is always an ongoing process.

Another interesting example of the confusing intersections between philosophy and strategy is in the area of peace and conflict resolution studies. An exponentially growing field within the high school districts and superintendencies nationwide, a growing number of non-school-based agencies are vying for Board of Education dollars to hire trainers to teach teachers and students how to become mediators. The problem with so many of these agencies is their interpretation of the nature of conflict itself. As one colleague who helped found and define the field of peace studies thirty years ago noted, "We developed this work to stir up some conflicts, not to resolve them!"[25]

Negotiating with the British for the full independence of India, Mahatma Gandhi himself noted that their interests and positions were in direct confrontation, though no violence was evident at the peace talks themselves. For many of the newer agencies, conflict resolution seems to mean little more than methods of getting people to stop arguing, to kiss and make up. Like some bad marriage counselors who refuse to look at society's sexist power dynamics in attempting to bring couples back together, these mediation mongers have little to offer in solving systemic problems. A temporary state of "not violence" is shallowly substituted for the principle of nonviolence — a soul force that recognizes the need to overcome institutional and individual oppression as a precursor to lasting peace.

From a purely strategic point of view, there is much to be learned in the field of education from the nonviolence practitioners and peacemakers. Whether or not we adhere to a philosophical position of pacifism, the power of nonviolence to overcome an "us-them," powerless-against-the-enemy mentality is vital indeed. In addition, militarism in any form — even in the name of radical change — needs to be critically examined and studied for its lasting effects and impressions, especially on youth.

The conflict resolvers who fail to look at the root (or radical) nature of the problems they attempt to address adhere to neither nonviolent nor progressive principles or practices. They are technicians with an apparently apolitical agenda, but one that insidiously supports any status quo. The powerful always have the upper hand, and the students or staff who become trained in these techniques get little more than tools to appease. At worst, these mediators will never be able to address long-term problems of any social significance, nor will they ever comprehend the nature of Banks's level-four goals.

When Linda Lantieri and Tom Roderick of Educators for Social Responsibility (ESR) developed the Resolving Conflict Creatively Program (RCCP) in the 1980s, they had in mind a deeper and sharper analysis of conflict, its causes, and possible school-based solutions. To their credit, New York's alternative schools were one of the earliest and most consistent supporters of these efforts on the high school level. Having expanded to a national program, RCCP trains thousands upon thousands of staff and students in well-grounded and interwoven conflict-mediation techniques, peace philosophies, and social change skills.[26]

New York's ESR Metro program has maintained a dynamic commitment to its own roots in the anti-nuclear weapons movement. A 1999 effort brought the alternative superintendency and ESR into a new partnership, as noted author Jonathan Schell and the Nation Institute initiated a campaign for nuclear abolition called Disarm 2000. Schell's 1982 *New York Times* best-seller, *The Fate of the Earth*, helped broaden the peace movement of the time,[27] and his research and writings in the late 1990s revealed that many top U.S. military officials had taken positions, at times quietly, against the continuation of the nuclear arsenal. To put this perspective into the U.S. history and global studies classrooms of New York, a curriculum was designed and a forum developed that was unveiled at an alternative schools conference in spring 1999. In addition to Schell and Admiral Stansfield Turner, Princeton physicist Zia Mian and Atlanta-based poet and grassroots activist Malkia M'Buzi Moore set the tone for coalition-building and school-based activism on this vital peace issue. M'Buzi Moore, principally a human rights campaigner who at the time was national coordinator of the YouthPeace program of the War Resisters League, made the point that "the movement for nuclear abolition needs to be inclusive of issues that are important to diverse communities."[28] This model was replicated on the national level the following fall, as the Consortium on Peace Research, Education, and Development (COPRED) — the nation's oldest peace studies network — brought this message to a national audience.[29]

As has been discussed, a unique component of the very structure of New York's alternative schools was their coalition nature. This fact, however, did not automatically guarantee that freshmen, seniors, assistant principals, school secretaries, and local community leaders from each of these sites worked together for positive programs. Coalition-building, in its essence, means a certain degree of ideological compromise. Sticking to one's principles necessitates a strategic understanding of the differences between what's ultimately desired and what's required to move in the general direction of that desire. Believing that we must work for peace and that peace is never just the absence of conflict but the active presence of justice, we can both build broad bridges and stay rooted in our own radical agendas.

ROOTED IN AN EFFORT TO LINK WITH COLLEAGUES ACROSS DISTRICT, NATIONAL, AND INTERNATIONAL LINES

The structure of the Central Board of Education of the city of New York, now officially the Department of Education, changed substantially between 2002 and 2004. Through the 1980s and 1990s, the minimally decentralized board worked through thirty-plus community-based K-8 school districts and six high school superintendencies, topped off by a seven-member body, which hired a schools chancellor to oversee the budget and run the system. Central Board's Office of Multicultural Education (OME), consistently one of the most forward-looking and educationally practical of the Brooklyn-based administrative offices, brought together multicultural coordinators and staff "turnkeys" from throughout the huge, five-borough bureaucracy. Alternative schools' support for OME was unwavering from the beginning, but the office has nevertheless had to shift and bend to the various political winds of the past years.

When Chancellor Joseph Fernandez first made a priority of multicultural education, albeit in an unstrategic and unsophisticated way, the official BOE statement defining the term was considered the best in the field. Using the phrase "education that is multicultural," New York's definition denoted the idea that "multicultural education" must always be more than simply an area of study within the educational landscape. Education, rather, could either be a space of Eurocentric and gender-blind thinking (i.e., not multicultural) or it could be a space for learning that is sensitive to and designed by and for a diverse and engaged population (i.e., education that is multicultural). New York State Education Department regent Sheila Evans-Tranum, then director of Alternative Schools' Auxiliary Services for High Schools, was one of the first proponents of this inclusive thinking, which, in its full wording, addressed issues of race, ethnicity, age, religion, gender, sexual orientation, and handicapping condition. It was used as a model for educational boards throughout the country; Mayor David Dinkins's vision of a "glorious mosaic" of cultures was being actively taken up in the schools.

Of course, all this was not without its problems. Fernandez's poor handling of politics and public relations in part contributed to the "Children of the Rainbow" debacle. A first grade curriculum suggested that some teachers might consider reviewing the growing field of children's books on gay and lesbian parenthood to broaden their own knowledge base and possibly to include them in the classroom if appropriate (say, in the instance where one of the students in class had "two mommies"). Some Afrocentric and Latino educators, concerned that their struggles for inclusion would be wholly subsumed amid the controversy of the gay agenda, became unwitting allies of white Republicans from Queens, who took their wrath out on Fernandez, characterizing him as misguided at best, heathen corrupter of youth at worst. By the time Fernandez suggested that condoms might be made available in high schools as a pro-health measure (after having apologized for and recalled the Rainbow curriculum), his career as chancellor was just about finished. The end of David Dinkins's one and only term as mayor was not far behind.

New York City's official policy regarding its overall relationship to its independent Board of Education did not begin to change substantially until the second term of Mayor Rudolph Giuliani. Like Republicans and Democrats before him, he wanted total control of the board to come under the purview of the mayor's office, with all the implied fiscal powers. One of Giuliani's chief differences, however, along with his penchant for an expanding and military-focused police force and his disrespect for communities of color, unions, youth, and critical thought in general, involved a willingness to exert a control over chancellors and board policy despite the administrative separation. Through overt and covert means, Giuliani made his presence felt, putting all educational reform efforts on the defensive.

The OME and policies supporting education that is multicultural were far from exempt from Giuliani's wrath. For a time, it seemed as if Chancellor Ramon Cortines's major relationship with the board's stated multicultural policy would be one of benign neglect. Brought in after Fernandez's ouster with Giuliani's support, Cortines was surely no spokesperson for unpopular causes. With a quiet deliberateness, however, he essentially maintained the strong emphasis on inclusion, committed to an antibias curriculum and a broad definition of diversity. Giuliani's own support, however, especially within the seven-member board that serves as boss to the chancellor, had grown. By early 1995, draft statements were written that would substantially weaken the board's official multicultural position and definition.

Separating its policy on multiculturalism from its policy on antibias education, the first Giuliani offensive was to take away the institutional nature of the concept of education that is multicultural. Simple curricular reforms, not the transformation of the total structure of schooling, became the focus. Secondly, the policy on multiculturalism — with broad outlines for teacher-training, curriculum development, and administrative support —

limited the definition of multiculturalism to three distinct areas: race, ethnicity, and linguistic groups. Finally, the new and separate policy on antibias education — which now included gender, sexual orientation, and the other groupings originally covered by the single, broad statement — was essentially defanged. Administrators and teachers were to make sure that these groups were not to be the subject of active hatred; the Central Board would do what it could to make sure that those groups were similarly not the focus of any proactive education and dialogue. Persecution of women, gays, religious minorities, and so forth was supposedly not to be tolerated, but those groups and their allies were also not to be in any way empowered or included in the work of the OME. For his part, Cortines made a statement against the changes before a February 15, 1995, vote that officially ratified these new and separate policies. OME director Leslie Agenda-Jones left the board in disgust the following June. In perfect Orwellian doublespeak, both policies were titled the "restrengthening of" multicultural and antibias education.

Under the able and careful direction of Evelyn Kalibala, the OME managed to survive these initial blows by putting together conferences, publishing book lists, and helping to network and provide staffing support for those still committed to the cause. Not so surprisingly — and for reasons far beyond their disagreement over multiculturalism — Cortines was pressured by Giuliani to leave, following an outrageous outing of Cortines himself as being gay. Dr. Rudy Crew, an African American man married to a white woman, seemed like a perfect symbol for Giuliani and a "why can't we all just get along?" position, but their partnership also dissolved, as Chancellor Crew ultimately supported multiculturalism and, more importantly, spoke up vehemently against a mayoral plan to station police officers in every high school. Ultimately, the underfunded and overburdened OME became the "Office of Multicultural Education/Social Studies," making official in New York the long-disputed proposition of national leaders in multicultural studies that the field be all-encompassing, especially focusing on math, English language arts, and issues far beyond any single content area. Fiscal year 2002 saw

Central Board monies for OME put mainly into an "academic intervention services" series — truly back to the basics.

Once an agreement was reached putting the BOE directly under the mayor's control, Republican mayor Michael Bloomberg dismantled the old board; replacing it was a streamlined department that grouped all schools, kindergarten through twelfth grade, into ten regional administrations. Though this restructuring, in and of itself, could not be criticized for attacking a clearly inefficient and ineffective bureaucracy, its effects on progressive education were quickly evident. By the spring of 2003, the OME had become the Office of Social Studies and Multicultural Initiatives; in July of 2003, the Alternative, Adult, and Continuing Education Schools and Programs were disbanded as a unified district. Though the strongest of alternative schools continue to exist under sometimes hostile regional bureaucracies, and the less strong programs maintained at a survival level within a special network, the power of a unified alternative force within the public education system in New York is gone.

This is not to suggest that all is as it should be beyond New York's troubled borders. The National Association of Multicultural Education (NAME), essentially a clearinghouse for pre-K through graduate school educators coming together for an annual conference of sharing best practices and business cards, has had its own problems. Though one could hardly compare the issues facing a relatively new professional organization with those of a major urban school system that has the budget of several small states, it has always been somewhat sad that NAME has not yet produced greater leadership within the overall national movement for educational justice and social change. One conference memory sticks out as symbolic.

At a southwest gathering full of excellent presentations from Chicano/Mexican-American, Native American, and African American educators and community leaders, two teacher-trainers of European descent were also featured, at different plenaries, as keynoters. Both of them had many published books and years of experience to their names. Both were well prepared and had many challenging antiracist stories to tell and perspectives to share. One, however, the older and more refined speaker, limited his remarks to calls for the most minor and short-term reforms. His speech, full of bravado and tales of the civil rights movement, was passionate, populist, and brilliantly orated; he was a credit to his race. The younger speaker — literally calling for a "revolutionary" multiculturalism, looking deeply at the need for structural and institutional overhaul and exercising an invigorating analysis of the connections between racism, sexism, classism, and the like — came out with fiery rhetoric, invoking Cuba's guerrilla hero Che Guevara. Unfortunately, he was all but incoherent, spouting terminology intended only for a tiny clique of highly academic, postmodernist, post-good-use-of-the-English-language minded.[30]

Those two speeches and the dilemma of NAME (and the creation of a vibrant and diverse national movement) signify an important lesson. Until we are able to evaluate the social upheavals of the 1950s through 1970s that gave birth to all the social change movements in the U.S. since that time, and until we are able to understand how to present propositions that get to the root of the problems of contemporary U.S. society in ways that the majority of people can at least comprehend, our efforts, organizations, and educational impacts will remain painfully limited and small. The fights for small schools, for empowering curriculum and environments, and for structures that reflect a full multicultural institutional overhaul are valiant and essential ones. New York's alternative schools have attempted to play some role in these fights, sometimes quietly, as is appropriate for community-based struggles, sometimes linking up across district and national lines. The good fight, however, can never be won in a single district or through a single initiative. The revolution in education that the U.S. requires will itself require a massive, creative movement. Until we can study successful movements both from within the U.S. and from around the world, we will be in no position to champion lasting change.

* * *

In reviewing the experiences of New York's experiment in alternative education, several case studies seem to typify both what went right and what needed improvement among these small schools in a big city. Speaking with four outstanding educators about their school-based reflections and visions revealed some common themes and needs. Three "good fights" — for the promotion of a social justice pedagogy, against standardized testing, and for administrative restructuring that deals with racism, sexism, and homophobia — epitomize contemporary campaigns that, when put together, begin to make up a progressive schools movement in the U.S.

One alternative schools teacher who has attempted to bring the lessons of past movements and the challenges of current struggles into her day-to-day classroom practice is Queens-based former Satellite Academy social studies teacher Jessica Shiller. A past organizer for ACORN (Association of Community Organizations for Reform Now) working at its Brooklyn school and at the Manhattan-based Bread and Roses High School, Shiller has also worked as an educational consultant and organizer on several critical social justice projects.

"I've learned a lot from trying to teach social justice issues with teachers and kids," noted Shiller, who reflected on the "internal problems" of dealing with less-than-cooperative colleagues. "It's frustrating when you think of teachers who you'd expect to be with you politically, who are not willing to do the work. I'm thinking now primarily about radical teachers who don't put into practice what they talk so much about. There are teachers in progressive environments who themselves are fearful of what other teachers might think and administrators who are unnecessarily afraid of taking risks. There are others who simply don't know how to teach about controversial subjects and who have not had enough training in basic methods and practices."

Before joining the alternative schools, Shiller was a major organizer of a citywide high school teach-in against the death penalty and focusing on the case of death row journalist Mumia Abu-Jamal. With several dozen schools and well over one hundred people participating, the teach-in was a success as far as getting information out to students and staff. Abu-Jamal's case

— an overtly political one due to the clear racism involved in his conviction and appeals[31] — is controversial because of his past membership in the Black Panther Party and current relationship with the Philadelphia-based MOVE organization. Despite the fact that those building for the teach-in were careful to create lesson plans and a historical context that would allow for critical thinking and dialogue, many were afraid to join the efforts in their initial stages. Though the alternative superintendency took no official position on this after-school activity, many schools — including the host site, Beacon High School — played a central role. An unflattering *New York Post* article on an initiator of the project based at one of the oldest alternative institutions, City-As-School, suggested that the entire movement for progressive education was made up of little more than apologists for cop-killers. Instead of taking a strong position against this typical yellow journalism, many administrators, even within the alternative superintendency, went on the defensive, weakening the effort.

More recently, a social justice concern that had been steeped in controversy took a turn in a new direction. Shiller described her part in developing curriculum and activities on the situation of the U.S. Navy bombings of Vieques, Puerto Rico. "First, in the context of a global studies class, we brought up Vieques as one of the clearest modern examples of imperialism. I went to an International Tribunal held on Vieques in November 2000,[32] and I wanted to bring that information back to the school. Along with other staff members, I helped organize a forum where I showed some of the video of the Tribunal and discussed with students their questions and perspectives. It was billed as a dual lunchtime/voluntary program: You'd learn about Vieques and be able to discuss U.S. policy implications."

Along with a number of Puerto Rican students at the school and with several other teachers who had traveled previously to Vieques, and at a time when growing newspaper coverage was fielding the issues of the ongoing Navy presence, Shiller found a receptive climate. Forty students showed up during their lunch period, and others joined at an after-school follow-up session. "There was a real charge that kids got from learning about something they had read about in the papers, something they already knew a little about, something that seemed relevant to them. They wrote letters to City Council members who had also traveled to Vieques, and some went to support demonstrations to stop the bombing. There was continued interest in the topic, as students continued to take part in related activities during the following academic year."

Without having to circumvent an administration that is, in Shiller's words, "fairly open to what we teach and how we teach it," the foundation for future work has been laid. By selecting an appropriate issue at an appropriate time, framing it in an educational manner and getting clear permission to proceed, Shiller and her colleagues were strategic in their dealings with the Vieques question. That Puerto Ricans of all political tendencies — from *independentistas* to commonwealthers to statehooders — had united in their demands for an immediate end to the bombing was also a point of some significance in building further support beyond the Puerto Rican community.

As far as ongoing social justice pedagogy and taking on controversial subject matter, Shiller is enthusiastic. "On a very basic level, once given the opportunity, students will begin to ask where and how else imperialism and injustice happen. It has been transformative for them to know that there are people out in the world doing things, trying to make a positive change. This made them want to get more involved and continue to be involved in issues where they feel they can make a difference."[33]

* * *

Beyond dealing with the crisis of irrelevant content, perhaps the leading area of concern today for U.S. educational progressives is the issue of standardization. Making a difference in the means by which students are assessed and evaluated is a significant focus of much activism and analysis. Marty Neill, the Boston-based executive director of FairTest, an advocacy organization for fair and open testing, correctly suggests that the definition of standards and reform itself is muddied within education circles. "Right now," Neill writes, "the governors' and business leaders' view of standards and testing is the centerpiece of what passes for educational reform."[34] Far from simply being off-center or on the wrong track, the very notion of standardization goes against the essence of high standards truly sought after by developing critical thinking skills.

There has never been a question or disagreement on the need for high standards for learning. The question of who sets the standards, however, is at the core of the current problem. "Even in the hands of sincere allies for children, equity and public education," notes Deborah Meier, "the current push for standardization…is fundamentally misguided. By shifting the locus of authority to outside bodies, it undermines the capacity of schools to instruct by example in the qualities of mind that schools in a democracy should be fostering in kids — responsibility for one's own ideas, tolerance for the ideas of others, and a capacity to negotiate differences. Standardization instead turns teachers and parents into local instruments of externally imposed expert judgment."[35] In a commentary on the ways in which standardization and rigidity under Mayor Bloomberg's administration was pushing more students to drop out, Fannie Lou Hamer Freedom High School principal Don Freeman noted that in the 1980s and early 1990s one was allowed to "focus on the kids." Writing after his retirement, Freeman asserted that in those days "the pressures were not the same, and you could take some risks. Now," he concluded, "you're supposed to focus on the numbers."[36]

One leader of the portfolio assessment methods among New York's alternative schools has been John O'Reilly, a former math teacher and United Federation of Teachers chapter leader at the highly regarded School for the Physical City (SPC). SPC was founded, in part, to foster "expeditionary learning" skills — where students would learn about the world by literally exploring it. O'Reilly, an adult education specialist with the City University of New York, came to SPC because of his interest in this educational approach. "The standards movement started kicking around SPC in 1997," O'Reilly recalls, "and many staff members tried to find ways to embrace the standards while also embracing alternative means of assessing what the students were doing. We were one of only three schools nationwide connected to Outward Bound in a notion of expeditionary learning, but the standards brought in another master — the Board of Education bureaucracy. Outward Bound, in turn, began to pull away. Standards started to destroy the community and vision that SPC had as an alternative school."

O'Reilly admits that, beginning in 1998, SPC's serious push for portfolio assessment earned it a waiver from the New York State Education Department. Along with thirty or so other schools, SPC had been able to stall the otherwise mandated Regents exams and joined in a consortium to "protect the waiver." SPC's "mission," to accept one-third high achieving, one-third average, and one-third "at risk" students, had, in O'Reilly's view, compromised the overall approach of the school. "The curriculum, slowly but surely," he noted, "must be converted from an inquiry-based model to an information-based drill-and-kill model. So far, the students who have had to take the English Language Arts Regents for graduation have had a 100 percent passing rate, and we'll do well in the Math Regents as well. Working under the principle that we'd eventually have to combine portfolio and Regents assessment, we developed an inquiry-based math curriculum in conjunction with the InterActive Mathematics Program of California. Cathy Wilkerson, a key person committed to transformative education, helped develop this link for us. But students will have a much harder time in the areas of science and social studies. Teachers' abilities to create rich activities will diminish, and we've already seen class size increase. We've prepared relatively well for the coming of standardization, but the school is still not as nurturing a community as it has been, could be, or will become."

Undoubtedly, the effects of standardized tests on a school like SPC will be less significant than in schools with higher rates of "at-risk" and learning-disabled students. The prediction that in several years the Regents exams or current standards will be "dumbed down" to allow for better statistical gains to be cited by next year's politicians do little good for those students who will never be able to earn a high school diploma this year. Schools that had the potential for excellence have been, without question, demoralized. O'Reilly himself took a leave from the school system at the end of 2001, just one of the many "fatalities."

When George W. Bush was selected as president of the U.S., the "Texas education miracle" began to be touted throughout the U.S. and abroad. With required high-stakes testing becoming the norm, teachers are pressured into tracking and teaching students according to their testing potentials. A two-decade veteran bilingual educator teaching in the Texas school system likened the process to scholastic Darwinism. Trapped into teaching to the test in order to keep her job, Teddi Beem-Conroy wrote — in the important national reform newsmagazine *Rethinking Schools* — that she found herself at the center of a twenty-first-century educational odyssey.[37]

"The demands that are put on teachers and students is extremely severe," reflected O'Reilly shortly after his resignation. "At SPC, the core group of teachers has largely left, with 30 percent of the teachers leaving annually. The focus on the larger questions — What is justice? What is gender? What is the quality of life in New York City? — was lost in the process of bending to the standards. These questions, which are unanswerable, are the really interesting ones for students to explore: the fundamental questions of life. In addition, our own knowledge of our students — what they have been struggling with most and least — is also lost or diminished in this process. With small, inquiry-based schools and performance-based assessments, there is a better chance for the majority of students to succeed, to show their development, their brilliance, and what they've learned."[38]

* * *

On the administrative level, the push to meaningfully address the issues of institutional racism, sexism, or heterosexism have been slow at best. While personal commitment and growth have taken place in certain areas, translating this to structural change and consciousness is another matter entirely. Two administrators, Susan Dean and Clint Jackson, have been attempting to work on that structural and group-consciousness level for some time, with some successes.

"The whole system needs a change — from the top down as well as from the bottom up," stated Dean, who has worked as a teacher in support services, at shelters and group homes, and in prisons. "To poor people, the school system has been a very oppressive place, and there must be more going into poor communities — in the form of grants, teachers, et cetera. In my dream, the difference is that the government will be giving out resources more equitably, and private enterprise will also have a role — so that students have a job and skills when it's time for them to go to work. I know I'm talking socialism here!...a decentralized, socialized education."

Ironically, Dean compared her dream of a radical restructuring with a reality from her childhood often thought of as reactive. "Let's talk about how my mother was educated, in a small town, taken care of by the community," she recounted. "They called it segregation, but the students learned. It was community-based education, where you're being taught by your own — like in a family — but it worked! I find that in the alternative schools, we do have a focus on the needs of individual students, more than students as a mass group. But there's still a 'great white male hope' attitude — even amongst administrators who are essentially progressive. Hard-working folks still don't take that extra step, not relating to certain problems — like ethnic stereotyping, benign neglect of certain populations, covert racism — that really do exist."

Largely because of this, Dean decided to go into administration, becoming an assistant principal at the Harvey Milk School for Lesbian, Gay, Bisexual and Transgender and Questioning Youth (HMS). HMS, in coordination with its parent program, the Hetrick-Martin Institute, developed exercises for staff that have enabled rethinking and frank dialogue about sometimes hidden homophobia within the teaching environment. One such exercise, where educators at high schools throughout the city were asked to choose between one of four phrases written on a blackboard, to stand up and say their name, and to then say the phrase, was a constant source of consternation. The phrases: "I am gay," "I am a lesbian," "I am bisexual," or "I am transgendered" were always met with snickering, shock, and a refusal in certain instances to participate. The idea of simply "saying the words" and putting oneself in another's shoes — if just for a second — created havoc and distress in most adult groupings. At times, this exercise has legitimately allowed lesbian or gay teachers to "come out" to their colleagues. At other times, nongay (or closeted) teachers have had long discussions about their own resistance and how these must affect their relationship to students who are actively questioning their own sexuality. The Harvey Milk School was founded not so much as a segregated space to teach lesbian and gay studies but as a safe space to teach students who were being attacked or ostracized in "normal" schools because they didn't fit the majority gender identity or sexual orientation model.

From Dean's viewpoint, the example of the Harvey Milk School fits well into a vision that struggles for diversity, pride, and enlightenment. "I want culture to become more a part of this educational process," she concluded. "Students who truly develop culturally have a great sense of pride — and so much else falls right into place. As an administrator, I plan to focus on staff development as one way to bring about realistic educational reform. In-house learning for everyone together — from principals to parents — can make a difference: the only way to truly improve student outcome."[39]

In the middle of the July 2003 summer break, the Harvey Milk School made national headlines as it shifted into its new DOE region, designated by its geographic locale. With a major grant for expansion and educational innovations, HMS faced substantial attacks from right-wing fundamentalists and civil libertarians alike. The protests were largely in reaction to HMS's success at providing a choice for students who simply didn't fit in at their zoned schools, as well as for simply serving the LGBT population in an explicit and unapologetic way. "Some school systems elsewhere, including in small Midwestern towns, have instituted programming for gay students in response to successful civil rights lawsuits brought by gay young people who were repeatedly harassed and beaten in school while the administration looked the other way," noted Andy Humm, Hetrick-Martin's founding director of education and a former member of the New York City Commission on Human Rights.[40] Mayor Bloomberg, having been elected in part with support from the lesbian and gay community, supported the school — though perhaps at the price of a more mainstream educational approach. Two of the first changes to take place once HMS "moved" to its new region was the replacement of Dean by a principal with ties to Wall Street and the letting go of all staff connected to the alternative schools or multicultural education. In the rush to ready the school for reopening with a 100 percent DOE staffing turnover, thousands of dollars worth of books from the old Alternative Superintendent's Multicultural Library were simply thrown away; one hopes that some of the philosophic foundations of that innovative school were not similarly discarded.

Career Education Center (CEC) assistant principal Clint Jackson, a colleague of Dean's, comes from a different historic vantage point, but he has ended up with similar political perspectives regarding the institutional hurdles facing transformative teaching. For twenty-eight years an operations manager at IBM, Jackson came into the school system to escape the corporate mentality. "What impressed me about the New York City Board of Education," noted Jackson reflectively, "was its lack of understanding about what its mission is. Somewhere down the line, the structure of the organization became more important than the mission — that students must come first. We have lost a sense of what we're attempting to do, with and for our students."

CEC is a multisited alternative program that has focused on education of homeless youth but includes many diverse partnerships with a variety of non-Department of Education agencies throughout the five boroughs. It is a microcosm of the superintendency itself. Although focusing largely on the Graduate Equivalency Diploma (GED) rather than the high school Regents diploma, CEC has had positive results in reaching students most often neglected by the school system as a whole. From this vantage point, Jackson discussed not just the alternative schools but the entire state of education today.

"Outside influences — not least of which is the business community — are attempting to dictate the educational agenda of this country," Jackson suggested. "Corporate America is sending us a message that we're not producing students that they can use. The irony of this is that those same corporations are unwilling to make any contribution to the furthering of positive educational goals. An investment in education in this country is not being made."

Corroborating Dean's analysis, Jackson admitted, "There is an institutional racism, sometimes subtle, when the capitalist agenda suggests that competition must be limited. Who is in the competitive pool — especially people of color — is what's being limited. If there's anybody within the system attempting to address the needs of those 'on the fringes,' it's people in the alternative schools. By our very nature, however, people think that we're talking about the academically challenged. In reality, what we're finding is that our students, many very bright, have certain needs — sometimes economic, sometimes medical, sometimes emotional. Oftentimes, these social needs are what make it difficult for a student to focus academically. Someone needs to stand up and say: 'Hold it. If our mission is to produce citizens who are able to contribute to society, then we need to understand that some groupings have been shortchanged by the system.' Raising the bar without addressing the problem — how to approach education so that it is meaningful for all — will simply create a new generation who will fall through the cracks."

As an administrator in a school with some of the neediest of students, Jackson can speak firsthand of how small class size, an understanding of multiple intelligences, and personalized support and assessment can empower and help motivate students. These experiences, however, are hardly replicated nationwide and may have little impact if the institutions in society outside of the field of alternative education are as unchanging as ever. "We must face the fact," Jackson stated directly, "that there were and are still folks in this country whose vested interests were never in agreement with the concept of 'Education for All.' We're talking about the maintenance of corporate structures based essentially on institutionalized racism. In this context, there is no incentive or desire to effectively teach our students creative thinking skills."[41]

* * *

From a personal narrative of the possibilities of reform to the hard economic and political realities of the difficulties of radical change, a single observation can summarize education in the U.S. today. Despite many positive instances of school-based alternatives, multiculturalism, and empowerment, on the whole young people are more needed as cogs in the machine or cannon fodder than as critical shapers of their own and our collective future. Education in this nation is in a downward spiral.

The remaining question is, of course, not how to mourn but how to organize. Examining the situations in South Africa and Eritrea is relevant because both of those countries have faced and continue to face seemingly insurmountable odds. The need to figure out the strategic political and economic actions needed to push for meaningful social change in the U.S. is as great today as it was over thirty-five years ago at the height of social upheavals. It is no less relevant here and now than it has been in situations where true revolutionary possibilities have appeared to be more imminent. One mistake of past generations was in believing that revolution in the U.S. was "just around the corner." Another, even more grievous error can result from a pessimistic worldview that suggests that such radical change in the U.S. can never come about and need never be prepared for. There were voices, indeed, who insisted that a true end of apartheid, or full independence for Eritrea, could also not come about, at least not in our lifetime.

The next generation cannot afford such ahistorical errors, be they rooted in utopianism or fatalism. We must remember the wise words repeated by South African Constitutional Court jurist Albie Sachs, a white ANC leader who was almost killed in an attack by apartheid forces in Mozambique. Revolutions, he reiterated, always seem impossible until they happen. Once they start, however, it seems like all along they were inevitable.[42] For progressive educators especially, and those involved in comparative education and historical review in particular, our priority must be in answering a single question: what must be done now to bring us together and move us forward as a viable, unstoppable force?

Conclusion

LEARNING FROM AFRICA — TEACHING ABOUT HUMAN RIGHTS IN THE U.S.

Time is tight. The pressure cooker that has always been a better analogy for American society than the melting pot has about reached its bursting point. Revolutionary change is needed now. Included in this revolution must be concepts fundamental to all revolutionary movements true to their name: a commitment to participatory, decentralized, and direct democracy; a commitment to equality and empowerment among diverse groupings; a commitment to human rights for all, including the right to live in a peace that is based on justice for all. Transformative education must serve as both a key toward achieving this liberating revolution and an inalienable right guaranteed by it.

The field of education, as I have tried to show through a number of examples, is in its own state of international crisis. Despite valiant attempts and meaningful reforms in local areas, there are few nation-states that can be cited as models for truly transformative learning. The effects of globalization, more appropriately understood as simply a "new face" of imperialism,[1] have been devastating worldwide, especially in the southern hemisphere. In the U.S., educational administrators at the top of their field are openly criticizing the Bush agenda. Following a June 2001 meeting, Michigan's superintendent of education Thomas D. Watkins, Jr., commented, "The federal government pays less than 7 percent of the overall education budget. If the tail wants to wag the dog, let's make sure the tail has a lot more financial resources tied to it….More mandates and calls for accountability without the corresponding resources is not helpful."[2]

For U.S. pedagogues to learn from our African counterparts, an entire shift of thinking must take place. As leading sociologist and past president of the International Peace Research Association Elise Boulding stated, "It's time to begin learning from Africa, not just about it."[3] Our own consciousness about internationalism, solidarity, and the give-and-take of a new world — opened to us in part by the technologies of the Internet and in part by the tenaciousness of the youth around us who are beginning to scream out for new answers to old, unresolved questions — must shift away from our Eurocentric models. We have barely begun to listen to our own colleagues — like Bob Moses or New York's Bernard Gassaway and Claudia Zaslavsky[4] — who have attempted to translate African lessons to the U.S. context. One colleague in the international nonviolence community suggested that even staunch U.S. anti-imperialists are overly self-focused. "We always want to be the best at being the worst!" she noted. We seem barely prepared to humble ourselves and become learners — not just teachers — on a world scale.

This is not to say that the examples of South Africa or Eritrea lend themselves to easy transference or suggestions for progressive U.S. educators. There is clearly much to criticize in the recent policies of both countries, with some points to emphasize as examples not to follow. Teacher-training in both nations has been sadly lacking and incomplete. And while the building of new schools in rural areas has been cited as an achievement of both countries, with unprepared educators and, in South Africa's case, an unclear curricular focus or, in Eritrea's case, overwhelmingly overcrowded classes, these new buildings may take years to be adequately utilized. In the words of one Pan-Africanist observer, "Too much has been attempted too quickly, without adequate planning. . . . If the curriculum and the teachers are good, I don't mind learning in a class taught under a tree!"

Nevertheless, there are lessons we can draw from this review of our African counterparts. The Pan-Africanists themselves point to a leading path for us all in the areas of ethnic studies and multiple perspectives. By viewing the world as one with many "centers," they suggest a new way of looking at ourselves and one another.

In South Africa, whatever the pains and problems of the national government's initiatives, the increased access to education for the most oppressed communities is a step we have at best half taken in the U.S. Though not put into full practice, that education is at least planned to be student-centered, a perspective only fleetingly adopted in New York schools and never fully acknowledged throughout the U.S. South Africa's attempts at outcomes-based assessment may seem similar to the standards movement here, but a careful look at the best of what OBET suggests incorporates the possibility for alternatives that is lacking in our more rigid national schemes. The idea implied by some educators in New York's alternative schools — that we must include both portfolio assessment and the state Regents in our sets of tools — is fully embedded in OBET's broad theoretical framework within South Africa. The teacher-training in South Africa that has been done successfully has almost always relied on a community-based center and perspective. This understanding of the role of elders and community leaders is too often lacking in even the most progressive of American alternatives. The most ambitious of South African reforms, an attempt to use traditional Africanist tools of healing and human interaction to make education a site for constructing a new society, may provide an inexact model for U.S. teachers. It is an experiment well worth watching, however, as our own American traditions of feisty resistance and rebellion need much revitalization.

Eritrea's examples seem based, first and foremost, on their continuing commitment to multilingualism and unity amidst diversity. The U.S. is miles behind a national movement that embraces difference in this fundamental way and have much to learn from a country that is struggling to put into practice a language policy that all of our own top researchers have long deemed most successful in creating a literate population. Eritrea's uneven achievements in education should in no way detract from their consistent attempts at social change. We have yet to begin to implement whole and primary language development models, still debating whether "English only" is a viable option in largely Spanish-speaking regions. U.S. education is similarly underdeveloped when compared to Eritrea in the area of teacher-student dialogical dynamics. This most fragile of Eritrean initiatives has been all but lost within the formal structures of post-independence *realpolitik*. The foundation, however, of teacher-as-learner and learner-as-teacher was laid in the most formative time of Eritrea's liberation movement and has not seen its last day. Dialogical and dialectical thinking, perhaps best evidenced today by the work of Eritrea's youth movement and by the open questioning of postwar national priorities, is an ambitious contribution that U.S. educators would do well to pay careful attention to.

As for an analysis or conclusion regarding progressive educational initiatives within the U.S., there is very little way to easily establish an answer to the question "What is to be done?" Learning from the "best of" practices of our contemporaries overseas is, at best, only half the battle. Fighting the "good fights" noted in the previous chapter, rooted as they may be in the principles established through our practice, is also only the first step in the direction we need to go. It has always been a particular and peculiar difficulty of the U.S. progressive movement to find broad points of strategic agreement. For educators, who must take some responsibility in leading the way to an understanding of how we may communicate with one another beyond our narrow niches, I would suggest that our next step be to look within.

In this instance, looking within must mean more than simply dealing with one's personal or even local issues. Though previous commentary has clearly underscored the importance of knowing oneself before going out to teach others, at this time an urgent task must be to look critically at the nature of the whole of contemporary U.S. society. Specifically, we must be willing to talk in our classrooms about human rights — and not simply human rights on an international scale. If we are not able to come to terms, as educators, with human rights violations currently taking place within the U.S., I fear that our future is a bleak one. Burrowing our heads in the sand, as we so often and cozily do without even realizing it, is an ultimately lethal solution. It is a lesson learned from experiences with the white community in South Africa during the days of apartheid. Some South African educators were at the forefront of attempting to break this dangerous cycle. In the U.S. today, we had better do no less.

Human rights violations in the U.S. must not be confused with injustices, which are ever-present in any society. The United

Nations Declaration on Human Rights,[5] taught in few classrooms and the focus of even fewer standardized tests, lays out some clear moral, political, economic, and cultural guidelines for appropriate behavior. Amnesty International's "Rights for All" campaign,[6] which turned the microscope on U.S. society in ways that organization has rarely done in the past, also points to some areas of critical engagement. The underlying, interconnected, and institutional basis of race, class, and gender discrimination and power imbalances in U.S. society make up the core of human rights violations on a large scale.[7] These are the issues, generally addressed as simple prejudices or nonsystemic personal idiosyncrasies, that lead to the majority of progressive, alternative, and multicultural reforms. In addition to broadening our understanding of the deeper, historical ways in which racism, classism, sexism/heterosexism, and militarism permeate the very basis of modern American society — the ways in which imperialism manifests itself internally and externally at the beginning of the twenty-first century — we must also make strategic choices.

As educator-activists, there are many ways one might choose to present the issue of human rights in a global (including U.S.) context. Two concrete areas of concern, however, seem well-suited to spotlight the rest. We must face the reality that political prisoners exist in the U.S., and that the U.S. maintains the world's last colony — Puerto Rico. Teaching about U.S. political prisoners and about Puerto Rico not only positions us to build a movement that will be based on the shoulders of past organizers and organizations, it also provides us with the tools to forge past our own realities and build alliances with constituencies and communities that the progressive educational sector has only paid lip service to. By taking the "bull by the horns," dealing directly with two of the most obvious and blatant U.S. human rights violations (nevertheless covered up by years of official denial and radical defensiveness), we introduce a core series of questions that provides a framework for future critical thinking skills and a life of inquiry and self-assessment. The student empowerment of which we so often speak can only come about with a clear, coherent, and historical view of the country in which we live.

Of course, there is a large menu of appropriate and important issues that must be worked on, taught about, and dealt with in building a powerful movement that will put "just plain folks" — and education — at the center of U.S. priorities. Strategic choices are hard to justify, and there is little benefit in placing hierarchies within the human rights arena. Ultimately, hindsight will reveal what key issues lead us to a new moment of social upheaval and the possibilities for lasting, positive social change. The reasons for selecting the "issues" of political prisoners and Puerto Rico, however, are many.

The vast majority of political prisoners today are elders and community leaders, purposely removed from sight to attempt a historical amnesia about the unfinished business of the civil rights and Black liberation movements. Though not forgotten by certain elements of the "left," and taken up by a growing number of college students and groups, these prisoners are the living history of our country's most recent attempts at social change — a history written down in almost no book or pamphlet.[8] Though Representative Cynthia McKinney shed some light on this topic during a fall 2000 "brain trust" meeting of the Congressional Black Caucus and some African American leaders at Harvard Law School and other prestigious institutions have begun to become more vocal,[9] the admittedly illegal policies of the U.S. counterintelligence program (COINTELPRO) have been largely successful in creating a climate whereby talking about the prisoners can make one appear a "conspiracy nut." The intensified repression of the post-9/11 era, manifested most dramatically in the Patriot Act, only makes the need for militant action and education more urgent.

The possibilities for students to uncover and review government documents; to write and engage in Q and A with elected officials, community members, and the prisoners themselves; and to research recent history that they can discuss with their own family members or older influences seem a much too rich set of curricular activities to pass up. In some ways, the lack of materials and textbook guidance available ensures that students must give careful review to primary sources and be taught to "read between the lines" and evaluate often conflicting commentary. It is a chance for nonstandard, inquiry-based education, with an opportunity for empowering political involvement and an exciting engagement with the historical process. The ultimate freedom of these prisoners — who serve disproportionately long sentences, often under draconian conditions — is also a moral imperative.

Puerto Rico's political status as a colony, only in part revealed by the example of Vieques, is a little-disputed fact but little-known reality to most Americans, even in those cities with large Latino populations. The people of the Puerto Rican nation are in relative agreement on this; from *independentistas* to commonwealthers to statehooders, they have traveled annually to the United Nations to seek ultimate redress of this pressing injustice. How the situation may be resolved — through incorporation, separation, or an adjustment of the status quo — is not agreed on by Puerto Ricans themselves; it is a question non-Puerto Ricans may well wish to steer clear of. But the reality of current colonialism, as defined and recognized by international law, exists most prominently in this appendage to the U.S. empire. Puerto Rico's status is confirmed when Puerto Rican males age eighteen and over may be drafted into the Armed Forces while at the same time are not able to vote in U.S. presidential elections; it is reconfirmed as all judicial matters on the island are conducted in a language foreign to most of its inhabitants. Widespread resistance is clear when mayors from small villages and the Catholic archbishop and functionaries from political parties, often aligned with the U.S. Republican Party, all agree on the same point — be it the need to free political prisoners or stop the bombing of Vieques or the use of Spanish as Puerto Rico's "national" language. It is evidence of Puerto Rican pride and patriotism, and not mere irony, that these are among the same points taken up by the men and women who spent twenty-plus years in jail for shooting at the U.S. Congress because of their nationalist convictions.

Modern colonialism in this postmodernist era is unheard of and embarrassing, yet few educated Americans know even as much about our own colonial entanglement as was described in the previous paragraph. That the people of Vieques had, by 2003, laid the foundation for an international movement that forced the U.S. Armed Forces to make a rertreat — even as U.S. imperialism vis-à-vis the Middle East is being overtly applauded by many Americans — is merely symptomatic of the strange problematic of modern empire-building. It demonstrates the fears in Washington, D.C., brought about by its colonial predicament. It is symptomatic of a situation that must inevitably, and significantly, change.

Educators, of all people, should be aware of these dynamics and ought to be prepared to make a positive contribution to this change. In regions of the U.S. where there are large Puerto Rican populations, apathy and ignorance are especially striking; in regions of the country where there is a thirst for justice and peace, there is also no excuse for inactivity.[10] The possibilities for exciting and enriching instructional modifications seem almost self-evident. One innovative math department collaborated with a Puerto Rican bomba and plena music specialist to create algebraic formulas and reinforce high-level fractional equations.[11] More typically, the poetry of Julia de Burgos or Juan Antonio Corretjer and the novels of Nicolosa Mohr or countless others are brought into the language arts and/or Spanish curriculum; social studies lessons may be developed for any number of high school courses. There are few drawbacks to these suggestions, most of which can even be easily applied within the context of a heavily burdened, "standardized" classroom. The benefits may include being able to hold one's head high when the question is asked: "Which side were you on?" The benefits may include helping to bring about some form of liberation in our own lifetime.

There can be little doubt that most people who go into the field of education do so with lofty goals, to play a positive role in the lives of young people, to "touch the future." In the process of making a lifelong commitment to a career in education, all educators are, in turn, touched by those same young people we are in place to serve. Sometimes that touch creates cynicism; sometimes it inspires innovations. Always there comes a time when teachers need recharging. A lifelong commitment to social change and social justice, not unlike the teaching profession itself, undergoes a similar process and requires a similar steadfastness in order to avoid burnout, disenchantment, and stagnation.

For educators involved with social justice and transformative teaching, the challenges are all the greater to keep focus on the larger picture and not be dismayed by the many small defeats.

An international perspective, always looking for some new approaches from far-flung but forward-looking corners of the globe, is one way to stay fresh and full of insight. Looking deeply at the most difficult but pressing issues — educationally and politically — is another way to maintain a strategic vision and understand that we are not in it alone and not without a striking past and a solid future. None of this work — of building an education for liberation and creating liberated spaces where enlightened education may take place — is easy. No one ever suggested it would, should, or could be. As U.S. freedom fighter Frederick Douglass once noted, "Power concedes nothing without a struggle. It never has and it never will."

Appendix

BEGINNING AGAIN:
WHOSE STANDARDS? AN AFRICAN TEST

As I stumbled back from a one-year sabbatical on the morning of September 5, 2001, the disorientation felt after a year of time structured solely around intellectual pursuits (and the a.m. schedule of a new baby son in my life) was severe. With a sense of accomplishment that at least I'd put down a first draft on my comparative study of transformative educational models, I survived that first week just barely and in a bit of a daze. Second week came, feet still dragging, morning routines barely falling into place. First thing Tuesday is our regular core staff meeting, and one teacher arrived a bit late, with news that several students were outside huddled around a radio. Seems a plane had accidentally crashed into one of the World Trade Center towers downtown....

Years later, it is still difficult to forget the horrible impact of those planes, but also disappointingly difficult to remember some of the more positive lessons of that day. We (New Yorkers especially) must remember how, after hours sitting glued to communal television sets, many of us first stumbled onto the streets of our city in the direction of hospitals and blood donor centers. We must remember that the makeshift memorials adorning all of our neighborhoods and centered in Manhattan's Union Square, were covered not only with the pictures of those lost but also with peace signs alongside the calls for revenge, of broken rifles and rainbows. We must remember that words like "survival" and "disorientation" live on in us with a different meaning — a different connotation — than they had before. We have been called upon to begin again. We must rebuild our movements for radical change. We must also rise to the challenges of new tests of our creativity, passion, and internationalism.

With those thoughts in mind, to end this book as I began it — in true Friday morning surprise-quiz mode — I present a test. Several students and staff joined together to form the following patchwork exam. It is a test all about standards and perspectives, but not the standards and perspectives typically held by the writers of high stakes tests and nationally constructed measures within the U.S. It's an African-centered test, and your failure could forecast the failure of our society to move beyond our present morass. Please take out a number-two pencil. Do not share your answers (or the questions) with your neighbor, domestic partner, colleague, or pet. Do not pass go or go online for answers. Please do not look to the back of the book for guidance, and by no means should you smile or show emotion. You have ten minutes.

From: African Action Position Paper: Africa's Debt (Ann-Louise Colgan, wwww.africapolicy.org, July 2001)

1. The 48 countries of sub-Saharan Africa's combined annual expenditure in the area of foreign debt repayment is
    a) approximately $13.5 billion.
    b) paid exclusively to rich foreign creditors for past loans of questionable legitimacy.
    c) termed by the All-Africa Conference of Churches "a new form of slavery, as vicious as the slave trade."
    d) all of the above.

From: Eritrean National Exam, Grade 7 History, June 2000:

2. In Africa, iron was first used in
    a) North Africa and Egypt.
    b) the south.
    c) central areas.
    d) the east.

3. The fall of the Songhai was caused by
   a) the conquest of Vandals.
   b) the attack by Morocco.
   c) slave revolts.
   d) weakening of trade.

From: Eritrean Secondary Education, Certificate Examinations, General Knowledge

4. The last Secretary General of the Organization of African Unity was
   a) Abedel Aziz Boutlefika.
   b) Moammar El-Gadhafi.
   c) Nelson Mandela.
   d) Salim Ahmed Salim.
   e) Blaise Compaore.

5. Among pastoral nomads, wealth is usually measured in
   a) goats and cattle.
   b) oxen and cows.
   c) animals.
   d) camels.
   e) none of the above.

6. Tourists are attracted to visit Tanzania mainly because of its
   a) wildlife.
   b) archaeological sites.
   c) historic sites.
   d) beautiful lakes.
   e) volcanoes.

7. Ngugi wa Thiong'o is an African writer from
   a) Nigeria.
   b) Uganda.
   c) Tanzania.
   d) Kenya.
   e) Ghana.

8. One of the following countries is highly dependent on food aid and is a recipient from the U.S.A. and the European Community.
   a) Eritrea.
   b) Libya.
   c) Kenya.
   d) Ethiopia.
   e) Mauritius.

9. Recently, integrated farming method has become popular in Eritrea because
   a) it uses modern technology.
   b) it uses production techniques that increase productivity.
   c) it helps farmers raise their productivity.
   d) it saves time and energy of farm households.
   e) all of the above.

From: Eritrean Secondary Education, Certificate Examinations, History

10. All of the following were aspects of the Mahdiyya movement in Sudan except one:
    a) It was against Anglo-Egyptian imperialism.
    b) It was only an anti-Christian movement.
    c) It conducted a campaign inspired by the life and preaching of the Prophet Mohammed.
    d) It aimed at expanding its influence over its neighboring states.
    e) It strongly criticized the Egyptian corrupted bureaucracy.

From: Career Education Center staff development exercise, 1999

11. Big Pun, the first Latino rap artist to go platinum, popularized the phrase
   a) "Viva Latina!"
   b) "Biruqa Unida."
   c) "Boriqua, Morena."
   d) "Tonight, tonight."

12. 411 is to Mary J. Blige as Hard Core is to
   a) Foxy Brown.
   b) Lil' Kim.
   c) Eve.
   d) Missy Elliot.

13. As two young women walked by, a group of guys exclaimed, "Bling, bling!" The above comment was probably making a reference to
   a) their detailed gold chains.
   b) their loud conversation.
   c) their raggedy clothes.
   d) their unusual hairstyle.

14. What do the "L," "L," and "J" stand for in LL Cool J's name?
   a) Last Love, Jack.
   b) Ladies Love, James.
   c) Long Lost, Joey.
   d) Lucky Lawrence, Jazz.

15. "It is we who are the civilized ones that are liars." This quote was written by
   a) Maya Angelou.
   b) Paul Dunbar.
   c) Nikki Giovanni.
   d) Langston Hughes.

16. "If I knew Black people were going to wear my clothes, I wouldn't have made them." This statement was made by which popular designer?
   a) Calvin Klein.
   b) D & Gabanna.
   c) Gucci.
   d) Tommy Hilfiger.

17. The R&B group noted for their song about Bill Clinton and the Monica Lewinsky affair was
   a) Escape.
   b) THC.
   c) Destiny's Child.
   d) Boyz 2 Men.

18. P. J. Patterson is the leader of
   a) The Blue Notes.
   b) Jamaica.
   c) Guyana.
   d) Ghana.

19. bustdown: smoke as
   a) cigarettes: weed
   b) back: bone
   c) share: buy

20. hangout: die as
   a) dangerous: secure.
   b) safe: inside.
   c) home: live.

ENDNOTES

Introduction: Education for Liberation

1. See Matt Meyer, ed., *Multicultural Voices in Action* (New York City Alternative High Schools and Programs, 1995), 67; see also *Towards Making Education Multicultural: A Manual for In-Service* (New York: Board of Education of the City of New York, 1996), 324-25.
2. See Project Reach, Ethic Perspectives Series (Reach Center, 180 Nickerson Street, Seattle, WA 98109, 1991), 1-3.
3. A good start to learn more if you are in this category is Jim Messerschmidt, *The Trial of Leonard Peltier* (Boston: South End Press, 1983).
4. George Carlin, *Napalm and Silly Putty* (New York: Hyperion, 2001), 116.
5. Noel Ignatiev, *How the Irish Became White* (New York: Routledge, 1995).
6. Karen Brodkin, *How the Jews Became White Folks* (New Brunswick: Rutgers University Press, 1998).
7. Imari Abubakari Obadele, *Foundations of the Black Nation* (Detroit: House of Songhay, 1975); see also Imari Abubakari Obadele, *The New International Law Regime and United States Foreign Policy* (Baton Rouge: The Malcolm Generation, 1996).
8. Some comparative study along similar lines has already been conducted, as in Clive Harber, *Education, Democracy, and Political Development in Africa* (Brighton: Sussex Academic Press, 1997).
9. Paulo Freire, *Pedagogy of the Oppressed* (New York: Continuum, 1970).
10. Ira Shor and Caroline Pari, eds., *Education Is Politics: Critical Teaching Across the Differences* (Portsmouth, NH: Heinemann, 1999).

11. Paulo Freire, *A Pedagogy for Liberation* (New York: Continuum, 1987), 48. Namibian educators have used the term "transformation" to describe the complete overhaul of their educational system, which took place after independence from South Africa in 1990. See P. S. Swarts, *The Transformation of Teacher Education in Namibia* (Windhoek, Namibia: Gamsberg Macmillan, 2003).
12. William Ayers, Michael Klonsky, Gabrielle Lyon, eds., *A Simple Justice: The Challenge of Small Schools* (New York: Teachers College Press, 2000), vii.
13. Per Norstrom, paper presented at the United Nations, 29 May 2001, Office of the Special Coordinator for Africa/LDCS.
14. Ibid., 6.
15. "Africa: The Facts," *New Internationalist* (Oxford), 326 (August 2000): 18.
16. Preparing for the 21st Century Through Education, Training and Work (Pretoria: South African Department of Education National Report, 1997), 17.

Chapter 1: "Outsiders" — Contemporary Education in the U.S.

1. George Fredrickson, *White Supremacy: A Comparative Study in American and South African History* (Oxford: Oxford University Press, 1981), xi. See also Andrew Offenburger, Christopher Saunders, and Christopher J. Lee, eds., *SAFUNDI: South Africa and the United States Compared: The Best of Safundi, 2003-2004* (SAFUNDI Publications, 2005). Finally, as more U.S. Citizens "discover" the wealth we have to learn from the South African people, more comparisons are being made. Arnetha Ball's *Multicultural Strategies for Education and Social Change* (New York: Teacher College Press, 2006) is one of the best and most relevant to this study.
2. Ibid., xiv.
3. Ibid., 247.
4. George Frederickson, *Black Liberation* (Oxford: Oxford University Press, 1995), 270.
5. See, for example, the classic Carter G. Woodson, *The Mis-Education of the Negro* (New York: AMS Press, 1933; republished Lawrenceville, NJ: Africa World Press, 1990).
6. Frederickson, *White Supremacy*, op. cit., 274.
7. Ibid., 275.

8. Ibid., 276.
9. Ibid., 278
10. Ibid., 280.
11. *A Simple Justice*, 14.
12. Ibid., 15.
13. Ibid., 13.
14. Makani Themba-Nixon, "School Choice and Other White Lies" (*Seeing Black* web column, May 17, 2001): 3.
15. Ibid., 2.
16. See Eric Mann, *Dispatches from Durban* (Los Angeles: Frontlines Press, 2002).
17. Themba-Nixon, *Seeing Black*, op. cit., 1.
18. "CFE Issues Analysis of High Court Decision," *Campaign for Fiscal Equity*, www.cfequity.org, July 24, 2003. Debates raged throughout the 2005 school year regarding the billions of dollars that Albany owed the New York City school system.
19. "When Jamas Is Enough: A Conversation with Gabrielle H. Lyon," *Simple Justice*, 131.
20. Kelly Kurt, "Tribes, Education Leader Debate Left Behind Act," Associated Press, October 31, 2005.
21. Jonathan Kozol, "Segregated Schools: Shame of the City," *Gotham Gazette*, January 16, 2006.
22. *A Simple Justice*, 34.

Chapter 2: We Have Our Voices: Eritrea in the Pre-independence Era

1. Les Gottesman, *To Fight and Learn: The Praxis and Promise of Literacy in Eritrea's Independence War* (Lawrenceville, NJ: Red Sea Press, 1998), 76.
2. Beehave Tekehaimanot, "Education in Eritrea During the European Colonial Period," *Eritrean Studies Review* 1, no. 1 (1996): 6.
3. As quoted in Bereket Habte Selassie, "From British Rule to Annexation," in *Behind the War in Eritrea*, ed. B. Davidson, L. Cliffe, and B. H. Selassie (London: Nottingham Spokeman Press, 1980), 58.
4. As summarized in Gottesman, *To Fight and Learn*, 44-47, 80-82.
5. Dan Connell, *Against All Odds: A Chronicle of the Eritrean Revolution* (Lawrenceville, NJ: Red Sea Press, 1997), 177.
6. Gottesman, *To Fight and Learn*, 34.

7. Ibid., 87.
8. Les Gottesman, "Hermeneutics of Literacy During Eritrea's War of Independence," *Eritrean Studies Review* 1, no. 2 (1996).
9. Gottesman, *To Fight and Learn*, 89-90.
10. Ibid., 179.
11. Ibid., 181.
12. Gottesman, "Hermeneutics of Literacy," 75.
13. Ibid., 227.
14. Ibid., 228.
15. Roy Pateman, *Eritrea: Even the Stones Are Burning* (Lawrenceville, NJ: Red Sea Press, 1998), 251.
16. Gottesman, "Hermeneutics of Literacy," 95.
17. Provisional Government of Eritrea, Basic Information on Education in Eritrea (Asmara: Department of Education, 1993), as quoted in Gottesman, "Hermeneutics of Literacy," 95.
18. Asmarom Legasse, "Traditions and the Constitution of Eritrea," *Eritrean Profile* (24 Sept. 1994): 3; as quoted in Gottesman, *To Fight and Learn*, 253.
19. Thomas Kennelly, "Let Eritrea Live," *Adulis IV* 3 (1987): 15; first published in the *Sydney Morning Herald*, 20 June 1987; quoted in Gottesman, *To Fight and Learn*, 260.

Chapter 3: Time Is Tight: Education in South Africa under Apartheid

1. Education for Affirmation: Conference Papers (Johannesburg: Skotaville Publishers, 1988).
2. Ken Hartshorne, *The Making of Educational Policy in South Africa* (Oxford: Oxford University Press, 1999), v.
3. Ibid., 9.
4. Ibid., 24.
5. Ibid., 26-28.
6. Human Sciences Research Council (1981), 14; as recounted in Hartshorne, *Making of Educational Policy*, 74.
7. *Education Is Ours: Working in the EWE Study Program* (Cape Town: David Philip, 1990), 9.
8. Ibid., 10.
9. Ibid., 39.
10. Ibid., 40.

11. *If You Want to Know Me: Voices from SOMAFCO* (Alice, Eastern Cape, South Africa: Lovedale Press, 1999), i.
12. Ibid., 111. See also the excellent Morrow, Maaba, and Pulumani, *Education in Exile* (Cape Town: HSRC Press, 2004).
13. Hartshorne, *Making of Educational Policy*, 105.
14. Ibid., 106.
15. Linda Chisolm, "The Restructuring of South African Education and Training in Comparative Context," in *Education After Apartheid: South African Education in Transition*, ed. P. Kallaway, G. Krauss, A. Fataar, G. Donn (Hartford: University of Connecticut Press, 1997), 94.
16. Ibid., 55.
17. Pam Christie, "Globalization and the Curriculum: Proposals for the Integration of Education and Training," in *Education After Apartheid*, 115.
18. F. J. Nieuwenhus, *The Development of Education Systems in Post-Colonial Africa* (Pretoria: Human Sciences Research Council, 1996).
19. Paul Musker, *Outcome-Based Education: Theory into Practice* (Cape Town: Nolwazi Educational Publishers, 1997).
20. Peter Kallaway, "Reconstruction, Reconciliation, and Rationalization in South African Politics of Education," in *Education After Apartheid*, 41.

Chapter 4: Positive and Negative Globalizations

1. Silvia Federici, George Caffentzis, and Outssania Alidou, eds., *A Thousand Flowers: Social Struggles Against Structural Adjustment in African Universities* (Lawrenceville, NJ: Africa World Press, 2000), 8.
2. Ibid., 9. A more nuanced reflection on the current state of the academy in Africa can be found in Akilagpa Sawyerr's *Challenges Facing African Universities: Selected Issues* (Windhoek, Namibia: Association of African Universities, 2002). Presented as a special paper at the 2002 Annual Conference of the African Studies Association, Dr. Sawyerr spoke of the "severe body blows" inflicted upon African universities by a variety of factors during the last quarter of the twentieth century. His conclusions concur with Federici and Caffentzis that neoliberal globalization was a primary cause of the "prolonged crisis" facing higher education on the continent.

3. *Academic Freedom and Human Rights in Africa* (New York: Africa Rights Watch, 1991), 17.
4. Ibid., 19.
5. *A Thousand Flowers*, 88.
6. Ibid., 96.
7. Patrick Bond, *Elite Transition from Apartheid to Neoliberalism in South Africa* (London: Pluto Press, 2000), 118.
8. Ibid., 216.
9. Ibid., 169.
10. Ibid., 168.
11. See Joseph Stiglitz, *Globalization and Its Discontents* (New York: Norton, 2002); and George Akerlof, *Der Speigel* (July 2003).
12. Carlo Mitton, "Public Education in a New World Order — Surviving the Politics of Greed," June 2001.
13. Ibid., 1.
14. Samir Amin, "Third World Forum — An Interview with Naima Bouteldja," *Z Magazine* (July/August 2003): 54.

Chapter 5: Pan-Africanism and Africanist Philosophies of Education

1. For an ambitious overview of this, see Molefi Asante and Abu Abarry, eds., *African Intellectual Heritage: A Book of Sources* (Philadelphia: Temple University Press, 1996).
2. See, for example, Arthur Schlesinger, Jr., *The Disuniting of America: Reflections on a Multicultural Society* (New York: Norton, 1993).
3. One of the most important is Cheikh Anta Diop, *Civilization or Barbarism: An Authentic Anthropology* (Chicago: Chicago Review Press, 1991).
4. W. E. B. Du Bois, *The World and Africa: Inquiry into the Part Which Africa Has Played in World History* (New York: Viking Press, 1947).
5. As documented in Kwame Nkrumah, *The Autobiography of Kwame Nkrumah* (Edinburgh: Thomas Nelson, 1957), and in *Revolutionary Path* (New York: International Publishers, 1973).
6. See Bob Fitch and Mary Oppenheimer, *Ghana: End of an Illusion* (New York: Monthly Review Press, 1968).
7. Kwame Nkrumah, *Neocolonialism* (London: Thomas Nelson, 1965).

8. See, for example, Bernard Magubane, *The Ties That Bind: African American Consciousness of Africa* (Lawrenceville, NJ: Africa World Press, 1990).
9. James Banks, *An Introduction to Multicultural Education* (Boston: Allyn and Bacon, 1993).
10. See, for example, Carl Grant and Christine Sleeter's *Turning on Learning: Five Approaches for Multicultural Teaching* (Columbus: Merrill, 1989).
11. This historic Harlem-based meeting, organized and videotaped by the New York City Alternative High Schools and Programs Committee on Multicultural Education, was held in collaboration with the All-African People's Revolutionary Party, May 8, 1998.
12. Ibid.
13. Julius K. Nyerere, as quoted in N. Q. Mkabela and P. C. Luthuli, *Towards an African Philosophy of Education* (Pretoria: Kagiso Publishers, 1997), 11; see also Haki Mathubuti, *From Plan to Planet: The Need for African Minds and Institutions* (Chicago: Third World Press, 1992).
14. Bill Sutherland and Matt Meyer, *Guns and Gandhi in Africa: Pan-Africanist Insights on Nonviolence, Armed Struggle and Liberation* (Lawrenceville, NJ: Africa World Press, 2000), 89.
15. Mkabela and Luthuli, *Towards an African Philosophy of Education*, 14.
16. Ibid., 26.
17. Ibid., 59.
18. John K. Marah, "Pan-African Education in the 21st Century," *African Link* 9, no. 1 (first quarter 2000).
19. Catherine Odora Hoppers, "African Voices in Education," in *African Voices in Education*, ed. Higgs, Vakalisa, Mda, and Assie-Lumumba (Cape Town: Juta Publishers, 2000), 1.
20. Herbert W. Vilakazi, "The Problem of Education in Africa," in *African Voices in Education*, 202-5.
21. Birgit Brock-Utne, "Language, Democracy, and Education in Africa," Discussion Paper 15 (Uppsala: The Nordic Africa Institute, 2002), 8.
22. Catherine Odora Hoppers, ed., *Indigenous Knowledge and the Integration of Knowledge Systems* (Claremont, South Africa: New Africa Books, 2002), 14.

23. John K. Marah, *Pan-African Education: The Last Stage of Educational Developments in Africa* (New York: E. Mellon Press, 1989), 21.
24. *Journal of Modern African Studies* 1, no. 3 (2003): 281-91.
25. Ibid., 23.
26. From private conversations between Dr. Angelou, Bill Sutherland, and the author, Winston-Salem, North Carolina, April 15, 2001.
27. As in above.
28. Matt Meyer, "Post-Independence Educational Initiatives in Mozambique and Zimbabwe: A Comparative Review" (master's thesis, Columbia University, 1985).

Chapter 6: An Additional "R": Reconciliation, Education, and Empowerment in Postapartheid South Africa

1. 1996 Report (Pretoria: South African Department of Education, 1997).
2. From a speech given at the opening of the Sithengile School, Claremont, June 22, 1996.
3. 1996 Report (DOE), 33.
4. Ibid., 18.
5. Ibid., 21.
6. From a speech to the Committee of University Principals, January 16, 1996.
7. *Preparing for the 21st Century through Education, Training, and Work* (Pretoria: South African Department of Education, 1999).
8. *National Strategy for Further Education and Training, 1999-2001* (Pretoria: South African Department of Education, 2002), 13.
9. *Getting Learning Right* (Witswatersrand: Joint Education Trust [JET], 1999).
10. Ibid., 108.
11. Ibid., 118.
12. Ibid., 119.
13. Schmidt, et al., *The Third International Mathematics and Science Study* (New York: TIMSS, 1997), 122.
14. *Getting Learning Right*, 122.
15. Ibid., 128.
16. Ibid., 131.
17. Ibid., 204.

18. *Annual Report 1999* (Pretoria: South African Department of Education, 2000), 8.
19. Ibid., 27.
20. Ibid., 63.
21. Jonathan Jansen and Pam Christie, eds., "A Very Noisy OBE: The Implementation of OBE in Grade One Classrooms," in *Changing Curriculum: Studies in Outcome-Based Education in South Africa* (Cape Town: Juta Publishers, 1999), 203.
22. Cliff Malcolm, "OBET Has Different Forms," in *Changing Curriculum*, 93.
23. Ibid., 103.
24. Haroon Mahomed, "The Implementation of OBET in South Africa: Pathway to Success or Recipe for Failure?" in *Changing Curriculum*, 169.
25. Jansen, *Changing Curriculum*, 207.
26. Ibid., 209.
27. Meg Pahad, "Outcomes-Based Assessment: The Need for a Common Vision of What Counts and How to Count It," in *Changing Curriculum*, 247.
28. Ibid., 255.
29. Ibid., 269.
30. Ibid., 274.
31. Cheryl Reeves, ed., *The Struggle to Teach* (Cape Town: SACHED Trust and Langman, 1994), 101.
32. Ibid., 104. Note use of first name only.
33. Ibid., 106.
34. Ibid., 108.
35. Ibid., 113.
36. Ibid., 172.
37. Mpati, Pease, et al., eds., *Give Us Voices!* (Mowbray: Kagiso Publishers, 1996), 1.
38. From Ira Shor and Paulo Freire, *A Pedagogy for Liberation: Dialogues on Transforming Education* (Westport, CT: Bergen and Garvey, 1987), and developed by Paulo Freire and Donaldo Macedo, *Literacy: Reading the Word and the World* (South Hadley, MA: Bergen and Garvey, 1987).
39. *Give Us Voices!* 17.
40. See Frank Smith, *Reading Without Nonsense* (New York: Teachers College Press, 1979), and also Frank Smith, *Whose Language?*

What Power: A Universal Conflict in a South African Setting (New York: Teachers College Press, 1993). See also Linda Chisolm and Jean September, eds., *Gender Equity in South African Education 1994-2004* (Cape Town: Human Sciences Research Council Press, 2005).

41. *Give Us Voices!* 37.
42. Ibid., 3.
43. Ibid., 12.
44. Ibid., 47-50.
45. Ibid., 60.
46. Ibid., 97.
47. Thobeka Mda and Steward Mothata, eds., *Critical Issues in South African Education — After 1994* (Kenwyn, South Africa: Juta Publishers, 2000), 162-69.
48. Ibid., 151.
49. S. Vally and Y. Dalamba, *Racism, "Racial Integration," and Desegregation in South African Public Secondary Schools: A Report on the Study by the South African Human Rights Commission* (Johannesburg: SAHRC, 1999).
50. Ibid., 60.
51. From private conversations between Dennis Brutus and the author, New York City, September 22, 1999.
52. From private conversations between Archbishop Tutu, Bill Sutherland, and the author, Cape Town, July 25, 1998.
53. Sutherland and Meyer, *Guns and Gandhi*, xi.
54. Maqhudeni Ivy Goduka, *Affirming Unity in Diversity in Education: Healing with Ubuntu* (Kenwyn, South Africa: Juta Publishers, 1999), 1.
55. Ibid., 4.
56. Ibid., 13.
57. Ibid., 31.
58. Ibid., 52.
59. Ibid., 69.
60. Ibid., 74.
61. Ibid., 90.
62. Ibid., 154; see also the work of Neville Alexander. "Unless the language issue is tackled expeditiously," he has written, "we are going to be squandering many more billions of rands to produce something like a fifty percent failure rate." (From *We Are Fiddling*

While the Country's Schools Are Burning (Cape Town: PRAESA, 2 Feb. 2001.)
63. Ibid., 155.
64. Ibid., 202.
65. From personal conversations with QPC director Jeremy Routledge, Cape Town, August 1998.
66. See Sutherland and Meyer, *Guns and Gandhi*, 195-97
67. From personal conversations between Zenzile Khoisan and the author, Cape Town, August 1998; see also Zenzile Khoisan, *Jakaranda Time* (Cape Town: Garib Communications, 2001).
68. Sasha Polakow-Suronsky, "Erasing History," *Colorlines* 5, no. 2 (Summer 2002).
69. *Education in South Africa: Achievements Since 1994* (Pretoria: South African Department of Education, May 2001), 1.
70. Ibid., 7. By the time of the 2002-2003 DOE Annual Report (Praetoria: SA DOE, 2003), Asmal asserted that the new period had seen the "most comprehensive and rigorous review" of public school financing and policy.
71. Ibid., 14
72. Kadar Asmal and Wilmont James, eds., *Spirit of the Nation: Reflections on South Africa's Educational Ethos* (Claremont: New African Education, Human Sciences Research Council, and the DOE, 2002), 50.
73. Ibid., 127. That change has taken place most notably from small-scale projects is also borne out in Clive Harber's *State of Transition* (Oxford: Symposium Books, 2001), 70-73.
74. Ibid., 201. Chisholm was central to a further analysis of class and social justice in South Africa's public schools, explored in the volume she edited entitled *Changing Class* (Cape Town: HSRC Press, 2004).
75. Ahmed Bawa, "For South Africa, Open Universities," Ford Foundation Report (New York: Winter 2004). This view is in contrast with the concerns that M'beki's commitment to educational expansion is, in fact, receding. See S. Jacobs and R. Calland, eds., *Thabo Mbeki's World* (Pietermaritzburg, South Africa: University of Natal Press, 2002). Somewhere in the middle of these two perspectives is Mamphela Ramphele, former vice chancellor of the University of Cape Town, now a managing director of the World Bank. "South Africa must hold a record with respect to foot dragging," she has written, "around higher education reform."

See K. Asmal, D. Chidester, and W. James, eds., *Mandela: From Freedom to the Future* (Johannesburg: J. Ball Publishers, 2003).
76. As quoted in Kadar Asmal, "Sixth Report on the Provinces to the President from the Minister of Education," Ministry of Education, Pretoria, 2002, page 64.

Chapter 7: Eritrea at Ten: Victories and Realities

1. President Isais Afwerki's Tenth Anniversary speech, May 24, 2001.
2. Gebre Hiwet Tesfagiorgis, ed., *Emergent Eritrea: Challenges of Economic Development* (Asmara, Eritrea: Red Sea Press, 1993), 48.
3. Ibid., 50.
4. Yegin Habtes, "Restructuring Education in Eritrea: Policies and Practices," in *Emergent Eritrea*, 60.
5. Joan Sullivan-Owomoyela, "New Wine in an Old Bottle: Culturally Relevant Curriculum from Eritrean Indigenous Systems," *Eritrean Studies Review* (Lawrenceville, NJ), 1, no. 2 (Fall 1996): 2.
6. Ibid., 7.
7. Ibid., 14.
8. While this point is further documented elsewhere, see also Miska Lebasi, "Prospect for Bilingual Education in Eritrea" (awate.com, April 25, 2001); and assorted papers from the Against All Odds Conference.
9. Sullivan-Owomoyela, "New Wine in an Old Bottle," 20.
10. Ibid., 24.
11. Dr. Belainesh Araya, *Counseling in an Eritrean Context* (Lawrenceville, NJ: Red Sea Press, 2001), 149.
12. Ibid., 148.
13. *Essential Education Indicators-1998/1999* (Asmara, Eritrea: Ministry of Education, 2000), p. 21.
14. *Eritrea: Basic Educational Statistics-1999/2000* (Asmara, Eritrea: Ministry of Education 2001), 12.
15. Interviews with Solomon Gaim, Kessete Kidawe, and Tsehaye Tsegay, held with the author in Keren, May 27, 2001.
16. From a discussion between the author and Father Angelo Regazzo, School Don Bosco, May 26, 2001.
17. Interview with Hailemariam Mehai and Dawit Kassa, held in Asmara, May 23, 2001.

18. Later Azeb Tewolde, the director of the Documentation Center, national archives of the independence struggle, gave us a full tour. Speaking of the substantial work she does with secondary student interns and visiting school groups, she insightfully commented, "We are trying to change the very culture of reading in society."
19. From an interview with the author, Asmara, May 28, 2001.
20. From an interview with the author, Asmara, May 25, 2001.
21. From an interview with the author, Asmara, May 28, 2001.
22. From an interview with the author, Asmara, May 28, 2001.
23. From an interview with the author, Asmara, May 24, 2001; see also Matt Meyer, "The Space of Peace and Freedom: Eritrea at Ten," *Peace News* (London) (Sept. 2001). See also Asmarom Legesse, *Oromo Democracy: An Indigenous African Political System* (Lawrenceville, NJ: Red Sea Press, 1992).
24. From an interview with the author, Asmara, May 28, 2001.
25. From an interview with the author, New York, May 5, 2004; see also Matt Meyer, "Breaking the Cycle," *Peace News* (London) (June-August 2004).
26. Tala Dowlatshahi, "Pathways to Reconstruction in Eritrea," *Choices* (New York), United Nations Development Program, 11, no. 4 (December 2002). There can also be no doubt that political and religious freedoms have been severely restricted, as outlined in the September 2003 news release and report from the International Secretariat of Amnesty International. In addition to their condemnation of the over-two-year incarceration of former top governmental officials and journalists, AI asserted that a few hundred others had been rounded up for their vocal criticisms of the ruling party, their conscientious objection to continued military service, and their religious beliefs. One disturbing portion of the report told of an August 2003 arrest of over two hundred children who were sent to Sawa military barracks under new education regulations and beaten for possessing Bibles. The International Conscientious Objectors Day, held annually on December 1, targeted the case of Eritrea in 2005. As part of coordinated worldwide educational efforts, the War Resister's International published a special report in *The Broken Rifle*, Newsletter #68. As reported in that issue, Eritrean Anti-Militarism Initiative founder Abraham Gebreyesus Mehreteab represented WRI in testifying before the United Nations Commission on Human Rights 61st Session, held in Geneva. He reported that "arbitrary detention, torture, deploy-

ment at the front line, forced labor—all without a hearing—have been common ways to punish deserters and objectors."

Chapter 8: Working within the U.S. Pressure Cooker

1. See John Stoltenberg, *Refusing to Be a Man* (New York: Meridian, 1989); see also Andrea Dworkin, *Life and Death* (New York: The Free Press, 1997), among many others.
2. See assorted writings and tapes of Dave Lippman, Urgent Records, PO Box 781, Chapel Hill, NJ 27514, www.davelippman.com.
3. For more on Oceanville-Brownsville and Bayard Rustin, see Jervis Anderson, *The Troubles I've Seen* (San Francisco: University of California Press, 1997).
4. For more details, see Sutherland and Meyer, *Guns and Gandhi*, 6.
5. As anyone familiar with the New York school system will intimately know, no one is actually laid off. Teachers become, in a poetically dismissive and disrespectful phrase, "excessed." This limbo state suggests that, somewhere in the huge five-borough, thirty-two-plus-district system there may be a job for you if you're willing to travel the distance and find the opening. Most good teachers, with options outside of the field open to them, take this as an opportunity to leave teaching altogether.
6. This friend, Rob Jones, a leader of the Columbia protests, went on to become program director at the American Committee on Africa. My leave, to attend a Gandhian conference in and travel around India, ironically took place at the same time that American Federation of Teachers president Albert Shanker was touring India with his friend Bayard Rustin. Interested in hooking up with one of his old cronies, Rustin decided to attend that same conference, the triennial of the War Resisters International. With some assistance from me, he met up with the young South African activists who had come out of their country at great risk. Rustin subsequently became an important supporter of these young South Africans.
7. The organizer of those protests, Tanaquil Jones, had also been a leader the year before in the anti-apartheid protests. She went on to take up the cause of political prisoners living in the U.S., eventually playing a pivotal role in the freeing of framed Black Panther Party leader Dhoruba bin Wahad, who spent nineteen years in jail before being granted unconditional release. Tanaquil was also a close friend of my future partner, Meg Starr, whom I first met at Columbia; Tanaquil and Dhoruba were married some

time later as well. Only one doctoral candidate walked out with us that day, a teacher by the name of Bill Ayers.

8. At Teachers College, Dr. Richard Streb bounced around at a frantic pace, firing off questions and strange bits of information about teaching and about the world, at a rate that even a seasoned New Yorker's ears could barely keep up with. He gave out goodies at every class and taught me much about infectious positive energy and timing. Lynn Chaleff, at Irving, had a calmness of spirit and deliberateness that could cut through the craziest of administrative blunders. A stickler for planning and preparation, she also provided a teacher's room where we could vent, chat, and mainly collaborate on classroom projects. Both Chaleff and Streb were old lefties, activists who took their causes into the field of education.

9. As originally reported in *Omni Magazine*, 1999, and noted in Shor and Pari, eds., *Education Is Politics*, 79.

10. For a more detailed history and analysis, see Charles E. Jones, ed., *The Black Panther Party Revisited* (Baltimore: Black Classic Press, 1998).

11. Joseph most recently cowrote and directed the film *Hughes' Dream Harlem* and is a founder of the Impact Repertory Theater.

12. Ture's principal organization, the All-African People's Revolutionary Party, still operates in several African countries as well as in Europe and the U.S. I first met him at the 1981 founding of New York's Progressive Campus Network, a group I helped initiate, when we fashioned a reunion between Ture and SNCC mentor Ella Baker, with both serving as keynote speakers. Later, Ture led a delegation to Libya, which I participated in, for a commemoration of the U.S. bombing of that country.

13. From the videotaped interview at his Harlem apartment, May 8, 1998.

14. The annual War Resisters League (WRL) peace award was given to Moses in 2001.

15. Robinson's social studies and English coteacher was none other than myself; our coordinator was Frank Carucci, who went on to become United Federation of Teachers Vice President for vocational education and the alternative schools network.

16. Robert Moses and Charles E. Cobb, Jr., *Radical Equations: Math Literacy and Civil Rights* (Boston: Beacon Press, 2001), 180-82.

17. See Philip Grevin, *Spare the Child* (New York: Knopf, 1986) for a shocking but important look at the devastating effects of ageism

in Western cultures; see also Lillian Weber, *Looking Back and Thinking Forward* (New York: Teachers College Press, 1997), which looks at some of the ways in which we can "follow after" even very young children.

18. Lev Vygotsky, *Mind in Society* (Cambridge: Harvard University Press, 1978).
19. The Waterways Project was one of New York City's most consistent literacy projects for students in the public high schools, publishing student poetry and prose and assisting teachers in developing authorship.
20. This process began at Career Education Center in 1990 and has since spread to other sites and schools, including an inspiring superintendency-wide annual student peace conference.
21. Several years later, Ingrid's life was tragically taken while on a peace mission to Colombia. New York educators and activists have tried to continue to honor her spirit in all the work that we do. For more information on the work of the Indigenous Women's Network, see also the Web site of another IWN founder, Winona LaDuke, http://voices.cla.umn.edu/authors/LADUKEwinona.html.
22. The Pedro Albizu Campos High School of Chicago is one of the many community-based initiatives that grew out of the work of that city's Puerto Rican Cultural Center.
23. From Luis Nieves Falcon, "Multicultural Education and a Pedagogy of Liberation," in *Multicultural Voices in Action*, 23.
24. Ibid., 26.
25. Dr. Joe Fahey, distinguished professor of religious studies at Manhattan College, is the author of numerous peace studies texts, including the seminal anthology *A Peace Reader* (Mahwah, NJ: Paulist Press, 1987). Though he has made this sort of remark in several public forums, this phrasing grew out a private conversation.
26. Linda Lantieri, *Waging Peace in Our Schools* (Boston: Beacon Press, 1996).
27. One million people from around the world converged on the United Nations and Central Park on June 12, 1982, for the largest peace and justice demonstration in U.S. history. As national representative of the Progressive Student Network and the United States Student Association, I began my own education about coalition building around that time. Jonathan Schell's *The Fate*

of the Earth (New York: Alfred Knopf, 1982) was the literary landmark that helped bring the issue to national attention.

28. The Nuclear Weapons Education and Action Project of Educators for Social Responsibility-Metro Area (NYC) was launched in December 1998. ESR Metro can be reached at 475 Riverside Drive, Room 554, New York, NY 10115, www.esrmetro.org.

29. Based at George Mason University, COPRED helped ESR first develop out of its subcommittee, the Peace Educator's Network. In a model of positive conflict resolution, COPRED and its main competitor in the field, the Peace Studies Association, have merged to form the Peace J Studies Association, now located at the University of San Francisco, www.peacejusticestudies.org.

30. NAME, 733 Fifteenth Street, NW Suite 430, Washington, DC 20005, www.nameorg.org, is still an important organization to join and build. Peter McLaren's *Che Guevara, Paulo Freire, and the Pedagogy of Revolution* (Lanham: Rowman and Littlefield, 2000), is well worth a read, despite this critique.

31. Not one to quickly condemn human rights violations in the U.S. or to take on the cases of political prisoners not specifically nonviolent in nature, Amnesty International has recently been in the forefront of critiquing Mumia's trial and appeals. See Amnesty International, USA, *A Life in the Balance: The Case of Mumia Abu-Jamal* (AMR 51/001/2000, February 17, 2000). See also Mumia Abu Jamal, *Live from Death Row* (New York: Perseus Book Group, 1995).

32. Luis Nieves Falcon, ed., *Violation of Human Rights in Puerto Rico by the United States* (San Juan: Ediciones Puerto, 2002). Serving under Dr. Falcon as chief assistant to the Tribunal judges, I was able to help bring together the various differing international perspectives on the legal ramifications of U.S. colonialism in Puerto Rico.

33. Interview with Jessica Shiller, New York City, June 26, 2001.

34. Kathy Swope and Barbara Miner, eds., *Rethinking Schools, Failing Our Kids: Why the Testing Craze Won't Fix the Schools* (Milwaukee: CRS, 2000), 116.

35. Deborah Meier, *Will Standards Save Public Education?* (Boston: Beacon Press, 2000), 24.

36. Nat Hentoff, "Testing to Create Dropouts? Playing the Number's Game for Kids' Futures," *Village Voice* (New York: 17-23 Sept. 2003); originally quoted in Tamar Lewin and Jennifer Medina, *New York Times*, 1 Aug. 2003; see also Wayne Barrett, "The

Underside of Bloomberg's School Reform," *Village Voice* (New York: 22-25 Oct. 2003).

37. Teddi Beam-Conroy, "Bamboozled by the Texas Miracle," *Rethinking Schools* (Milwaukee), 16, no. 1 (2001): 5. On the national level, critiques of the Bush No Child Left Behind agenda intensified when the state of Connecticut, led by their Republican governor, filed a lawsuit against the federal government late in 2005. Likening Bush to "a bully on the playground," Connecticut Education Committee cochair Andrew Fleischmann noted that the Bush initiative called for greater testing without providing greater resources for the state's school system (Norman Gillespie, Associated Press, Connecticut Challenges No Child Left Behind Law, Aug. 22, 2005). The continuing Bush-Bloomberg devastation of New York City schools has been highlighted by longtime education and trade union activist Maurice Gumbs, writing in the September 2004 issue of the online journal *Footnotes* that "the senior management team" of the New York City Department of Education "stands out as an eyesore, an embarrassment, and an affront to the parents of New York City's predominantly Black and Latino population. It is the symbol of a colonial-type Department of Education." While the mainstream meedia lauded the successes of the few new schools opened under Bloomberg (see David M. Herszenhorn, "In New York's Smaller Schools, 'Good Year and a Tough Year," *New York Times*, Aug. 8, 2005). Critic Nat Hentoff correctly noted that while test scores in some districts were rising, Black kids and white kids were getting different diplomas (Nat Hentoff, "Testing Bloomberg and Klein," *Village Voice*, June 22-28, 2005). In the May 24, 2005, edition of *Footnotes*, Maurice Gumbs charged Bloomberg and Klein with being "political pedophiles," stating that "it is the fault of useless elected officials that a Republican Mayor and a lawyer with no educational background have taken over the public schools and have now turned the children of these schools into a political commodity."

38. Interview with John O'Reilly, New York City, July 2, 2001. With Bush reelected in 2004, the situation in this and other areas grew dimmer. Coinciding with the monumental fiftieth anniversary of the Brown vs. Board of Education U.S. Supreme Court decision outlawing segregation in U.S. schools, educational analyst S. E. Anderson likened the situation to losing a fifty-year war of "educational genocide" for Black children (*Our Times* [Brooklyn], 9, no. 9. The January 2006 New York State Global Studies

Regents Examination seemed to underscore Anderson's point, in a passage on "two ways the British improved the lives of Africans." In perfect Orwellian doublespeak, the reading uncritically focused on the ways in which colonialism was more beneficial then harmful to the majority of Africans.

39. Interview with Susan Dean, New York City, June 27, 2001.
40. Andy Humm, "The Harvey Milk School," *Gotham Gazette* (New York: Citizen's Union Foundation, August 8, 2003), 5.
41. Interview with Clint Jackson, New York City, July 2, 2001.
42. Albie Sachs, *The Soft Vengeance of a Freedom Fight* (Berkeley: University of California Press, 2000), 210.

Conclusion: Learning from Africa: Teaching about Human Rights in the U.S.A.

1. See James Petras and Henry Veltmeyer, *Globalization Unmasked: The New Face of Imperialism* (London: Zed Press, 2001).
2. Tiffany Danitz, "State School Chiefs Concerned About Details of the Federal Education Bill," www.stateline.org, June 22, 2001.
3. Sutherland and Meyer, *Guns and Gandhi*, ii.
4. Claudia Zaslavsky is a math specialist, author of (among other important titles) *Africa Counts* (Westport, CT: Lawrence Hill, 1979). Bernard Gassaway, a former student at Brooklyn's Sterling High School, served as Superintendent of the post-2003 defunded and divided Alternative High Schools before resigning in disgust. Since his resignation, he has become an outspoken critic of the current state of educational affairs, and author of the inspiring *Reflections of an Urban High School Principal* (Jamaica: XenoGass ALG, 2006).
5. The best U.S.-based organization to find resources directly relating to internationally based human right's principles is the National Center for Human Rights Education, PO Box 311020, Atlanta, GA 31131, www.nchre.org. Its founder, Loretta Ross, was a keynote speaker at an annual COPRED/PSA conference in 1999, where she urged hundreds of assembled educators to simply read, review, and teach the International Declaration of Human Rights.
6. See Amnesty International, USA, *U.S.A. — Rights for All* (AMR 51/054/1998, October 1, 1998). They couldn't have been clearer: "The USA was founded in the name of democracy, political and legal equality, and individual freedom. It has established many institutions to protect individual civil liberties and played a key

role in the development of international human rights standards for the protection of all people. However, the USA is still failing to deliver the fundamental promise of rights for all."

7. On race and education today, see Louise Derman-Sparks, *Teaching/Learning Anti-Racism: A Developmental Approach* (New York: Teachers College Press, 1997); she is also the editor of the essential Anti-Bias Curriculum. On sexism, see Sadker and Sadker, *Failing at Fairness: How America's Schools Cheat Girls* (Farmington Hills, MI: Gale Group, 1994). On class, see Tamara Sober Giercek, *Teaching Economics As if People Mattered* (Boston: United for a Fair Economy, 2000).

8. This seems unbelievable, but is literally true. Howard Zinn's excellent and much-touted *A People's History of the United States* (New York: Harper and Row, 1984) doesn't include them, and the numerous histories of the 1960s and 1970s are also wholly inadequate. It's no wonder that textbooks make no mention of this "denied truth." See *Can't Jail the Spirit* (Chicago: Committee to End the Marion Lockdown, 5th ed., 2002); see also, for some background on related politics, J. Sakai, *Settlers: The Mythology of the White Proletariat* (Chicago: Morningstar, 1989).

9. A key organizer of this forum, both a central participant in and chronicler of this history, is Kathleen Cleaver. See Cleaver and George Katsiaficas, eds., *Liberation, Imagination, and the Black Panther Party* (New York: Routledge, 2001) for more background; see also David Gilbert, *No Surrender* (Montreal: AG Press, 2003). New scholarship is currently being developed in this area, most notably in Joy James, *Imprisoned Intellectuals: America's Political Prisoners Write on Life, Liberation, and Rebellion* (Lanham: Rowman and Littlefield, 2003).

10. Paulo Freire protégée Antonia Darder, with specific references to the inequalities afforded Puerto Ricans, has put it this way: "Teachers must become more cognizant of the alienating conditions faced by poor ethnic communities — conditions that are indelibly linked to historical events that position members of subordinate populations very differently from members of the ruling class." See Antonia Darder, *Reinventing Paulo Freire: A Pedagogy of Love* (Boulder: Westview Press, 2002).

11. The musician was Pepe Castillo, who can be heard on such CDs as *Banana Land* and *Jolope*, as well as on the special CD accompanying the children's book, Meg Starr, *Alicia's Happy Day*

(New York: Star Bright Books, 2002); the schools were Career Education Center and the School for the Physical City.

Appendix: An African Test

The citations for Questions 1 through 10 are included in the text.

Answers: 1 (d), 2 (a), 3 (b), 4 (d), 5 (a), 6 (a), 7 (d), 8 (d), 9 (e), 10 (b).

Questions 11 through 20 were developed by the CEC Committee on Multicultural Education, with special assistance from Adam Cooper and the students of Youth Leadership/Youth Fair Chance.

Answers: 11 (c), 12 (b), 13 (a), 14 (b), 15 (d), 16 (d), 17 (a), 18 (b), 19 (c), 20 (c).

INDEX

A Thousand Flowers 39
Abu-Jamal, Mumia 145
accountability 18, 19, 69, 77, 157
Addis Ababa 28
Affirming Unity in Diversity in Education 86, 119
Africa Watch 41
African National Congress 63
Afrikaans 32, 33, 59, 87
Afwerki, Isaias 30
Akerlof, Joseph 44
Algebra Project 130
Alidou, Oussania 39
alternative education 34, 51, 52, 74, 145, 154
Amharic 25, 29
Amin, Samir 43
Amnesty International 161
Angelou, Maya 57, 171
apartheid 9-11, 13, 14, 16, 20, 31-38, 42-44, 59, 60, 62, 67, 68, 72-74, 78, 81, 82, 84, 87, 125, 155, 160
Arabic 24, 25, 28, 97, 106, 112
Araya, Belainesh 98
asha bandele 134
Asmal, Kadar 65, 89, 90

Asmara 27, 28, 98, 100, 101, 103, 109, 111, 113
ASPIRA, Inc. 19
assessment 7, 17, 42, 65, 67, 68, 70, 71, 90, 91, 98, 110, 116, 148, 149, 154, 159, 161
Association of Community Organizations for Reform Now (ACORN) 145
at-risk 127, 149
Auxiliary Services for High Schools 140
Ayers, William 8

Bailey, Thomas Pierce 14
Balkanization 51
Banchiesi, Franco 42
Banks, James 85
Bantu education 31, 32, 72
Bawa, Ahmed 91
Beacon High School 146
Beatles 121
Bengu, S.M.E. 59, 62
Benin 52
Biko, Steve 89
bilingualism, multilingualism 23, 28, 115, 159
Bing-Wade, Margaret 130

Black Alliance for Educational Options (BAEO) 18
Black Panther Party 146
Black Power 53, 129
Black-Jewish relations 5
Bloomberg, Michael 143
Boer 32
Bond, Patrick 42
Botha, P.W. 31, 81
Boulding, Elise 158
Bread and Roses High School 145
British Military Administration 24
Brooklyn 119-121, 139, 145
Brutus, Dennis 82
Bush, George W. 20, 44, 150, 157

Caffentzis, George 39
Campaign for Fiscal Equity (CFE) 18, 19
Cape Town 72
Career Education Center 153, 170
Carlin, George 4
Center for Collaborative Education 20
Changing Curriculum 69
Children of the Rainbow 140
Chisolm, Linda 37
Christian National Education 32, 33, 72
Christie, Pam 69
Citizens for Peace 113
City Kids 129
City University of New York 148

City-As-School 146
Cliffe, Lionel 27
Coalition School for Social Change 137
colonialism 24, 26, 135, 163
Columbia University Teacher's College (TC) 124
Committee for Academic Freedom in Africa (CAFA) 39, 41
competency 77
Congress of South African Trade Unions 90
Congressional Black Caucus 162
consciousness 4, 14, 51, 53, 74, 81, 84, 111, 150, 151, 158
consensus 65, 70, 72, 81, 115
Consortium on Peace Research, Education, and Development 139
constitution 19, 74
Constitutional Court 60, 155
Coptic 25
Corretjer, Juan Antonio 164
Cortines, Ramon 141, 142
Counseling in an Eritrean Context 98
The Courage to Lead 77
Counter Intelligence Program (COINTELPRO) 129, 162
credentials 90
Crew, Rudy 142
Critical Issues in South African Education-After 110 34
Cultural Assets Rehabilitation Project 108
curriculum 1, 7, 24, 27-29, 35, 49, 58, 60, 62-64, 66-70, 88, 91, 96, 103, 105, 132, 133,

138, 140, 141, 144, 146, 149, 158, 164
Curriculum 2005 60, 62, 64, 66-68, 88, 91
Curriculum Development Institute 28

Darling-Hammond, Linda 16
Darwinism 150
Davidoff, Sue 77
de Burgos, Julia 164
De Lange Commission 33
Dean, Susan 150
DeGrasse 19
Dekemhare 101
de-linking 43
democracy 8, 9, 35, 54, 56, 88, 90, 109, 110, 148, 157
Dergue 25, 26
Derman-Sparks, Louise 85
Dinkins, David
Disarm 2000 138
dissent 32, 116
divestment 44, 125
Don Bosco Technical Training School 102
Douglass, Frederick 165
Du Bois, W.E.B. 49-52, 55

E.R. Murrow High School 121
Each Working in Education (EWE) 34-36
Edison Schools, Inc. 45
educational philosophy 7, 54, 88
Educators for Social Responsibility 138
Emergent Eritrea 95, 96

empowerment 35, 37, 52, 54, 57, 59, 61, 64, 97, 155, 157, 161
English Only 104
Eritrea: Even the Stars Are Burning 29
Eritrean People's Liberation Front (EPLF) 25-30, 93, 105, 106, 109, 110, 112
Eritrean Research and Documentation Center 105
Ethiopia 23-26, 29, 53, 93, 113, 116, 170
ethnicity 3, 30, 51, 73, 140, 142
evaluation 42, 90
Evans-Tranum, Sheila 140
expeditionary learning 149

FairTest 147
Falcon, Luis Nieves 134
Fannie Lou Hamer Freedom High School 148
The Fate of the Earth 138
Federici, Silvia 39
Fernandez, Joseph 140
Ford Foundation 91
Fredrickson, George 13
Freeman, Don 148
Freire, Paulo 7, 8, 75, 126

Gandhi, Mohandas 43
Garvey, Marcus 51
Gassaway, Bernard 158
Gauteng Institute for Curriculum Development (GICD) 68, 71
Gebreselassie, Beraki 29

gender 3, 9, 23, 60, 84, 104, 112, 114, 115, 119, 140, 142, 150, 152, 161
gender equity 9, 60, 104, 115
Gerahto, Tesfamicael 28
Getting Learning Right 63, 65, 66
Ghana 50, 52, 57, 58, 169, 172
Giddings, Paula 83
Giroux, Henry 75
Giuliani, Rudolph 141, 142
Give Us Voices! 74, 75
globalization 10, 39, 40, 42-45, 53, 56, 90, 131, 157
Goduka, Maqhudeni Ivy 83, 88, 119
Gold Coast 50
Gottesman, Les 29
Graduate Equivalency Diploma (GED) 153
grassroots 7, 41, 63, 67, 70-72, 81, 100, 113, 116, 129, 138
Guevara, Che 144
Guinea 50, 75
Guinea-Bissau 75
Guns and Gandhi in Africa 82

Habtes, Yegin 96
Haile, Reeson 30
Hartshorne, Ken 31
Harvard 29, 49, 113, 162
Harvey Milk School 151, 152
Hetrick Martin Institute 151
HIV/AIDS 9, 115
How the Irish Became White 4
Human Resources Administration (HRA) 130-132

human rights 10, 67, 80, 81, 91, 116, 139, 153, 157, 159-162

ideology 86
Ignatiev, Noel 4
immigrant 14
indigenous 3, 14, 40, 54, 56, 83, 96-98, 113, 134
informal education
Institute on Race and Poverty 91
International Education Development (IED) 124
International Monetary Fund 38
International Peace Research Association 158
Italy 24

Jackson, Clint 150
Jagger, Mick 122
Jansen, Jonathan D. 69, 70
Jeffries, Leonard 49
john powell 91
Joint Education Trust 63
Joseph, Jamal 129
Juta 77, 79

Kalibala, Evelyn 142
Kallaway, Peter 37
King, Jr., Martin Luther 2, 21, 50, 58, 86
Kiswahili 55
Kozol, Jonathan 20
Ku Klux Klan 17
Kunama 97
Kush 52
KwaZulu 32, 67, 73
Kweli, Talib 134

LaDuke, Winona 3
Lakota 85
Lamb, David 134
Lantieri, Linda 138
Legasse, Asmarom 29
Libya 23, 24, 52, 170
Lindamichellebarron 134
Lisante, Tim 133
literacy 7, 16, 19, 23, 26-28, 36, 49, 52, 62, 74-76, 95, 97, 100, 112, 115, 129, 131, 133
Luthuli, Albert 43, 54, 55
Luthuli, P.C. 54, 55

Mahmud, Saleh 26
Mahomed, Haroon 68
Malcolm X 2, 58
Malcolm, Cliff 68
Mandela, Nelson 34, 74, 82, 169
Mandela, Winnie 81
Mao Tse Tung 50
Maputo 124
Marah, John K. 55-57
Marcos, Ayn Alem 27
Mass Democratic Movement 34
Massawa 109
Mbeki, Thabo 65
McKinney, Cynthia 162
Mda and Mothata 79
Meier, Deborah 20, 148
Mekonnen, Yemawe 109
Mendefera 103, 105
Mesgina, Hailemikael 107
Meyer family: Simon Meyer, Marilyn 121
Mian, Zia 138

Ministry of Education (MOE) 96, 98-100, 102, 107, 109, 111, 115
missionary education 31
Mitton, Carlo 45
Mkabela, N.Q. 53, 55
Mkhatshwa, Smengoliso 63
Mohammed, Osman Saleh 111, 116
Mohr, Nicolosa 164
Moore, Malkia M'Buzi 138
Moses, Bob 129, 131, 158
Motshabi High School 78
MOVE Organization 146
Mozambique 124, 155
Mpumalonga 67
multicultural 1-4, 14, 51-53, 55, 76, 109, 128, 133-136, 139-144, 153, 161
Multicultural Voices in Action 134
Multilateral Agreement on Investment (MAI) 44
Muslim 24, 25
Myers, Walter Dean 134

Napalm and Silly Putty 4
National Alliance of Black School Educators 130
National Association for the Advancement of Colored People 50
National Association of Multi-cultural Education (NAME) 143, 144
National Education Crisis Committee 73
National Party 38

National Qualifications Framework Structure 90
National Union of Eritrean Youth and Students (NUEYS) 114, 115
Native American Indians 2, 3, 14, 119, 143
Negritude 51
Neill, Marty 147
Neocolonialism 50
New World Order 45
Nieto, Sonia 16
Nkrumah, Kwame 49
No Child Left Behind 20
Non-Governmental Organizations (NGOs) 113
nonviolence 43, 82, 86, 127, 137, 158
nuclear 44, 138, 139
NYC Board of Education (BOE) 140, 143
NYC Department of Education (DOE) 152, 153
Nyerere, Julius 54

O'Reilly, John 148
Oceanhill-Brownsville 5
Odora-Hoppers, Catherine 56
Office of Multicultural Education (OME) 139-143
Office of Population Census 87
Omaar, Rakiya 41
Open Learning Pathway Trust 74, 76
Organization of African Unity 25
Outcome Based Education (OBE) 67, 68
Outcome-Based Education and Training (OBET) 67-71, 88, 159
Outward Bound 149

Pahad, Meg 70
Palestinian 91
Pan Africanism 44, 45, 49, 51, 52, 130
Pan Africanist Congress 34
Pan-African Education 56, 57
Pateman, Roy 29
Patriot Act 162
peace education 86
pedagogy 7, 30, 35, 36, 66, 69, 73, 85, 114, 145, 147
Pedagogy for Liberation 7
Pedagogy of the Oppressed 7
Peltier, Leonard 3
People's Front for Democracy and Justice (PFDJ) 109, 110
portfolio 148, 149, 159
propaganda 115
Puerto Rico 8, 134, 146, 161, 162

Quaker 89, 120

race traitor 5
Rafto Prize 116
Reardon, Betty 86
reconciliation 59, 61, 81
reconstruction 15, 28, 42, 49, 77
Reconstruction and Development Program (RDP) 42
Regazzo, Angelo 102
Regents Exams 6, 149

Resolving Conflict Creatively Program (RCCP) 138
Rethinking Schools 150
Revolution Schools 95
Riker's Island 127, 133
Robinson, Mimsie 130
Roderick, Tom 138
Rustin, Bayard 121

Sahara Protests 44
Said, Edward 91
Satellite Academy 145
Schell, Jonathan 138
School for the Physical City 148
segregation/Jim Crow 13-16, 20, 151
Selassie, Haile 24, 25, 57
Senghor, Leopold 51
Sergeant Pepper's Lonely Hearts Club Band 121
The Shame of the Nation 20
Sharpeville 32
Shengeb, Mohiadin 114
Shiller, Jessica 145
Shor, Ira 7
Simmons, Esmerelda 134
Simon Hebe High School 74
Singer, Beverly 134
slavery 13, 15, 18, 20, 119, 168
Smith, Frank 75
solidarity 50, 51, 91, 111, 158
Solomon Mahlango Freedom College (SOMAFCO) 36
Somalia 23, 24
Souljah, Sister 134
South African Committee for Higher Education (SACHED) 34, 72-74, 76, 80, 89
South African Communist Party 34
South African Council of Churches 34
South African Defense Force 34
South African Department of Education (DOE) 59, 60, 62-67, 69, 71, 77, 80, 88, 90
Soviet Union 23, 25
Soweto 31, 32, 36, 72
standards 21, 66, 70, 79, 90, 114, 147-150, 159, 167-169
Sterling High School 122
Sterling, Louise 77, 79, 123-126, 132
Stiglitz, Joseph 44
Stokely Carmichael/Kwame Ture 53, 122, 129
Student Nonviolent Coordinating Committee 53
Sullivan-Owomoyela, Joan 96-98
Sutherland, Bill 43, 57
Sutherland, Efua 58
Sutherland, Esi 58

Tanzania 36, 53-55, 57, 130, 169
Taylor, Nick 63
Tesfagiorgis, Hiwet 95
Tesfagiorgis, Paulos 116
Tesfai, Alemseged 105
testing 44, 70, 145, 147, 148, 150
Themba-Nixon, Makani 17, 18
Third International Mathematics and Science Study (TIMSS) 64

Third World Forum 43
Tigrinya 24, 25, 30, 97, 99, 106, 112
Tirisano 65
To Fight and To Learn 26
Toure, Sekou 50
Towards an African Philosophy of Education 53
township 32, 72, 74, 78, 81
Truth and Reconciliation Commission (TRC) 81-83, 89
Turner, Stansfield 138
Tutu, Desmond 81

U.S. Department of Labor 127
Ubuntu 83, 84, 86, 88
Umlazi College for Higher Education 74
United Democratic Front 33, 73
United Federation of Teachers 121, 148
United Nations 6, 9, 39, 56, 80, 117, 163
University of Asmara 98, 101
University of Durban-Westville 42
University of the Western Cape 77
University of Wits 69
Upper Volta 44

Vieques 146, 147, 163
Vinjevold, Penny 63
vocational education 90, 95
Vulani Project 74, 76

War Resisters League 139
Washinawatok, Ingrid 134

Washington Irving High School 125
Watkins, Jr., Thomas 157
White Supremacy 4, 13, 16
Wilkerson, Cathy 149
William E. Grady High School 121
Winfrey, Oprah 91
World Bank 39, 42, 50, 91
World Peace Brigades 44
World Social Forum 43

Xhosa 32, 34, 59, 79, 83, 84, 87

Yohannes, Zemhret 110
youth 17, 53, 57, 81, 94, 95, 97, 98, 104, 114, 115, 129, 138, 140, 141, 151, 153, 158, 160

Zanzibar 54
Zaslavsky, Claudia 158
Zero School 26, 27, 29
Zimbabwe 58, 124